M000160254

"Garofalo has written something that is a unique, concise, yet po
tent tool in addressing one of the greatest challenges to modern
Christianity: religious pluralism. This book is a great resource for
campus ministries, with middle and high school students, and the
church. *All Roads* is a vital resource for the Christian community in
the new age as an inoculation against the false belief in a one-world
religion. Its timing is perfect."

    - Josh McDowell

       Founder, Josh McDowell Ministry

       Author, *The New Evidence That Demands A Verdict*

"As a Korean War veteran my father taught me there is no such thing
as an atheist or agnostic. He said an atheist is just someone who has
not been in the heat of battle during war time. He said, "Son, when
you are laying in a fox hole and the bombs are dropping all around you
and you can literally hear the bullets whizzing over your head. I've
seen grown men curl up into a ball and cry out to their Mothers, Jesus,
God or all three at the same time." In an era of political correctness,
religious pluralism, and revisionist history writing, Steven Garofalo's
All Roads Don't Lead to Heaven is timely and refreshing as it embold-
ens the faith-based community to speak the truth and power of the
Gospel and jump into the heat of the culture war in America. It is a
must read and primer for those of us in this epic battle to restore truth
and return our nation to a moral and free society. I plan on giving it
as gifts to all my loved ones caught up in false doctrines and atheism,
and to encourage those brethren weary in the good fight of faith."

    - Lonnie Poindexter

       Host, Lion Chasers with *Lonnie Poindexter Radio Show*

       Urban Family Communications / President, Lion Chasers
       Network

"This book is like a Primer – a small book used to teach a student to read or a short introductory book on some subject - except the content, in this case, is about proactively persuading others, as the author says, "of the exclusive truth of God's Word and His design for our life." Possibly the most famous Primer was the McGuffey Reader of the 19th century. This book is under another title, but I think it would be most appropriate to call it Garofalo's Primer on the Exclusivity of the Gospel of Jesus Christ. I have never read anything so comprehensive on the subject, yet so succinct. Whoever masters the arguments made here will become a master in helping others find the one true God and the one true road to heaven."

> - Dr. Mark Creech
>   Executive Director, Christian Action League of North Carolina, Inc.
>   Pastor for over 20 years

"Steven Garofalo has done a service to the body of Christ in providing a concise and readable refutation of the religious pluralism and relativism that seems to permeate our day—largely as a result of the New Age penetration of western society. He provides convincing arguments—biblical, logical, and historical—as to why we ought to trust the biblical account of Christ's exclusive truth claims, and, by contrast, why we ought to reject the claim that all religions lead to God. Highly recommended."

> - Ron Rhodes, Th.D.
>   President, Reasoning from the Scriptures Ministries
>   Author of over 70 books, including *The End Times In Chronological Order*

"Millions of people in our world today believe there are many paths to God. Steve Garofalo provides a logical and biblical refutation of the prevailing philosophy of religious pluralism. He also provides a biblical case for the exclusive truth of Christianity. This book will equip you to be able to answer the popular arguments of pluralism in our society."

- Kerby Anderson,
  President, Probe Ministries International
  Host, *Point of View radio talk show*
  Author of numerous books, including *Moral Dilemmas*

"Solomon exhorts us to *"buy truth and do not sell it"* (Proverbs 23:23). Today many base their beliefs on their feelings or preferences rather than on reason and truth. In a concise and compelling way Calvary member, Steven Garofalo, demolishes false views, and presents the uniqueness of Jesus as the only way of salvation. This book will strengthen the faith of followers of Jesus, and encourage others to take a fresh look at the evidence."

- Dr. John Munro,
  Senior Pastor, Calvary Church, Charlotte, NC

"Steven Garofalo has made an offering to God in his work, "All Roads Don't Lead to Heaven." He had used his God-given gifts and wisdom to present a work which is desperately needed in our American culture. While so many of us have recognized the quickly changing landscape of knowledge and understanding in this generation, nothing has been more consequential than people not understanding how critical their worldview is in shaping the culture of a nation. This book, a strong and concise read, gives a great introduction to anyone of where the battlefield is actually found in what has come to be known as the Culture War. Whether it be the origin of humanity, the sacredness of human life, or the foundation of marriage and sexuality, all of these will be viewed, and our beliefs about them determined by our worldview.

I am grateful for Garofalo's commitment to see people come to know Jesus Christ as Savior, Redeemer, and King. I believe this book will help anyone looking to share their faith, or seeking to understand why they look at and make sense of the world the way they do."

- Dr. Mark Harris,

Senior Pastor, First Baptist Church, Charlotte, NC

"In his book, *All Roads Don't Lead to Heaven*, Steven demonstrates the unique ability to simplify deeper concepts and ideas about truth and religious pluralism, and make them accessible for everyday use in *café conversation*. He tackles religious pluralism by dissecting its core fallacies and taking readers through a series of questions that are on the minds of most people about God, Heaven, truth and religion. For anyone who has a passion to take the church out into the community and to the urban meeting places in our society to engage people one-on-one, right where they are or in small group conversation, *All Roads Don't Lead to Heaven* is a must read and easy to use resource."

- Daniel Cotter,

Outreach Pastor, Open2Talk Urban Seekers Ministry

"My journey and studies into apologetics started over 20 years ago. *All Roads Don't Lead To Heaven* is a unique resource that pulls all the essentials of Christian apologetics together in a book that fits into your back pocket. This resource will lead people to the Truth about God, and equip you to more effectively share your faith in the New Age."

> - Dennis Gillikin.
> Executive Pastor, Encounter Christian Center, MD

"In an age of quick social media updates, our culture has grown accustomed to reading things in short intervals—on the bus ride, waiting in line, or simply after you put the kids to bed. Knowing this, Steven Garofalo has strategically condensed a response to the overly-used, under-examined belief that all faiths lead to the same point. Like any good exercise routine, it's best to start with something small and gradually work your way up from there. This book does just that. It is a great starting point for addressing the topic of relativism, and it also drives a beam into the ground for helping the reader to build an overall solid foundation for their faith."

> - Kent Suter
> Youth Pastor, Cornerstone Bible Church, Lilburn, GA

"Garofalo's book simplifies the issues related to religious pluralism in America and the apologetics tasks associated with them. *All Roads Don't Lead to Heaven* is itself like a road map that guides the reader through explanations of how Christianity genuinely differs from other world religions and its important uniqueness. Any Christian living in a multi-cultural environment or on a college campus will find it informative."

> - J. Thomas Bridges, PhD.,
> Academic Dean, Southern Evangelical Seminary, Charlotte, NC

"Steven Garofalo rings the bell with this concise contribution. In less than a hundred pages, he addresses the problem of pluralism as well as the fallacy of New Age mysticism. Garofalo cuts through the smoke and fog of false thinking to the bedrock of truth, absolute truth.

For many years, I have asked university freshmen if anything is true for all people, at all times, in all places. Never has one student admitted acceptance of absolute truth. It is to this millennial generation that Garofalo addresses his apologetic.

First, the depth of this little book is impressive. Despite the brevity of his presentation, the author spares no detail in constructing his case for truth. He faithfully shows C.S. Lewis' trilemma of Jesus, who must logically be a liar, a lunatic, or lord of the universe. From page one, this little volume engages the mind of the reader.

Second, the breadth of Garofalo's argument is impressive. He does justice to the New Testament documents, and he also marshals contemporary first century literature, such as Josephus. He presents the powerful argument of fulfilled prophecy, an ironclad proof of biblical assertion. Finally, he demonstrates the empirical evidence of manuscript multiplicity, showing that the New Testament is supported by more manuscript evidence than all other ancient documents combined.

Third, the brevity of this little book demonstrates the value of conciseness. Garofalo summarizes the case for theistic truth, while excluding extraneous data. It is a perfect read for both the friends and foes of biblical theism. I urge you to buy a few of these valuable little books and use them as a witness tool."

- Wayne Detzler PhD.,
　　Emeritus Dean & Distinguished Professor of Cross-Cultural
　　Apologetics
　　Southern Evangelical Seminary, Charlotte, NC

ALL ROADS DON'T LEAD TO HEAVEN

*Discovering God in
the New Age*

STEVEN GAROFALO

FOREWORD BY DR. NORMAN L. GEISLER

TRIEDSTONE PUBLISHING COMPANY

CHARLOTTE, NC

Editor: Jerri Menges

Cover design: Steve Mast

First printing 2016

Printed in the United States of America

Unless otherwise noted, Scripture references are from *The Holy Bible*: *New International Version*. ® Copyright © 1973, 1978, 1984, 1986 by the International Bible Society.

Scripture references marked NASB are from *The New American Standard Bible*® Copyright © The Lockman Foundation 1960, 1962, 1963, 1968, 1971, 1972, 1973, 1975, 1977, 1995. Used by permission.

Scripture references marked ESV are from *The Holy Bible, English Standard Version* ® Copyright © Crossway Bibles 2001, 2004. Used by permission.

Scripture references marked ESV are from *The Holy Bible, English Standard Version* ® Copyright © Crossway Bibles 2001, 2004. Used by permission.

Library of Congress Cataloging-in-Publication Data
Garofalo, Steven
All Roads Don't Lead To Heaven: discovering God in the new age / Steven Garofalo
Includes bibliographical references
1. Christianity and pluralism. 2. Pluralism. 3. Apologetics. 1. Garofalo, Steven. (Steven Garofalo),

ISBN 9780989744621 (TPB: Alk. Paper)
2. ISBN: 0989744620
Library of Congress Control Number 2016912588
CreateSpace Independent Publishing Platform
North Charleston, South Carolina

In memory of my good friend Todd Greenwood. As we sat in Johns Hopkins Hospital in Baltimore, MD, with one of Todd's kidneys already shut down and the other one shutting down due to his level 5 cancer, I asked Todd, "How are you in your soul?" He said "fine." I asked again—looking him in the eye, "How are you in your spirit?" He knew what I was asking him and he responded by propping himself up with all his strength, using both of his elbows. Taking off his oxygen mask, he gave me two thumbs up, and said, "I am ready to go home." Todd extended his arm from beneath his hospital bed sheet, palm wide open. I placed my hand in his hand and he closed his grip in Kung-Fu fashion, not letting go ... saying nothing, but saying everything about his love for God and for me. A few days later, Todd took the exit ramp to the true road into Heaven.

Until we meet again!

In Memory of Todd Greenwood
Monday, December 19, 1966-Tuesday, February 20, 2007

Jesus said, "In my father's house are many rooms. If it were not so, would I have told you that I go to prepare a place for you? And if I go and prepare a place for you, I will come again and will take you to myself, that where I am you may be also. And you know the way to where I am going." ... "I am the way and the truth, and the life. No one comes to the Father except through me." ... "Because I live, you also will live."
—Jesus Christ, John 14:2-6, 19, ESV

Contents

FOREWORD

If you are seeking a bold, direct, and forceful attack on the pluralism and relativism of our times, look no further. This is it. Steve Garofalo musters both logical and biblical arguments in favor of the exclusive claims of Christ. But he does not reason in a vacuum. He does so against the backdrop of the most widespread form of pluralism in our times—the New Age Movement.

There are three great enemies of absolute truth in our times: relativism, pluralism, and naturalism. The first two deny the absolute and exclusive nature of truth. The last denies all supernatural truth. All are fatal to Christianity.

The author of this book takes the first two head on. He demonstrates that the pluralistic claim that "all religions are true" is both logically and biblically unsound.

Logically, it is self-defeating to claim that pluralism is true, for that implies that all non-pluralistic views (e.g., exclusivism) are false, since the opposite of true is false. But if this is so, then even pluralism is making an exclusivistic claim. In short, pluralism hangs itself on its own gallows!

Further, the author demonstrates that all religions cannot be true since they teach opposites. But two opposites cannot both be true. Only one can be true while its opposite is false. For example, if it is true that God exists (theism), then it is false that God does not exist (atheism). Or, if there are many gods (Polytheism), then it cannot be true that only one God exists (Monotheism). Likewise, if Christ is the only way to God (exclusivism), then there cannot be many ways to God (Pluralism).

Biblically, the author makes a strong claim for the exclusive truth of Christianity. For Christ made the unique claim: that He was the only way to God. Strong historical evidence is mustered to support this claim. If it is true, then Jesus alone claimed to be and was demonstrated to be the Son of God and the only way to God.

So, popular as it may be, the pluralistic New Age view of God does not stand the test of either logic or Scripture. Steve Garofalo brings together in one short but penetrating volume a decisive critique of the most popular pluralism of our times. Few have tackled this important topic in a more consistent and biblical manner in such a short space.

—Dr. Norman L. Geisler
July 2016

ACKNOWLEDGMENTS

This book could not have been written without the incredible contributions of godly men who invested in me over the years, and the collaboration of many people. Men like Dr. Norman Geisler, Dr. Wayne Detzler, Dr. Ron Rhodes, Josh McDowell and Kerby Anderson. My wife, Heather, and our three children are a constant, immeasurable source of support. They give up time with husband and daddy, which they knew was necessary in order for me to research, write, and put together the pieces shared within the pages of this book. I cannot say enough about my good friend and editor Jerri Menges. This book would not have come together as it has without her. Thank you, Jerri.

I would also like to give thanks to two important men who serve on the board of ReasonForTruth.Org.—Michael Keating, Chairman; and Kent Suter, Vice President. These men stand with me day in and day out, providing immeasurable wisdom and direction for the mission at hand. A special thanks to Michael Keating for taking the time to read the entire manuscript as an extra set of eyes. And, finally to the many Christian brothers and sisters in Christ who reviewed the book and offered suggestions for its improvement and support for its mission. For that I am grateful.

Steven Garofalo

INTRODUCTION

ALL ROADS DON'T LEAD TO HEAVEN

"Rivers, ponds, lakes and streams—they all have different names, but they all contain water. Just as religions do—they all contain truths."—Muhammad Ali[1]

In the prime time television series, *The Story of God*, Oscar-winning actor Morgan Freeman sets out to probe humankind's deepest questions about God, religion, and life: Where do we come from? Who is God? What happens after we die? Do all roads lead to Heaven? Freeman interviews a carefully selected hodgepodge of historians, archeologists, and teachers of various world religions who would support his conclusion prior to this journey into faith. For Christians with a strong biblical worldview, Muslims with a strong belief in the Quran, and adherents of other religions, this six-part series will prove to be frustrating in part because Freeman fails to answer the questions he proposed. Instead, he concludes that all religions lead to the same spiritual Truth; that is, to the same God. The belief that multiple religions all lead to the same spiritual truth is called religious pluralism, and it is prominently on display in today's society.

That COEXIST Bumper Sticker

Most of us have seen the COEXIST bumper sticker, with each of its letters bearing the symbol of a different religion. We spot them on cars as we pull into a parking lot, or on cars that pass us on the street. What does this bumper sticker mean? Is it commanding all religions to coexist? Or is it simply proclaiming that all religions already do coexist and therefore lead to the same spiritual truth?

Religious pluralism is a growing view that comes with our increasingly multi-cultural world. It is a view that our kids will encounter in school, at college, in our neighborhoods, and in the workplace. While this view is not taught in most churches, it is preached from the pulpit of public opinion and the media. On June 15, 2015, Oprah Winfrey announced the weeklong landmark television series *Belief* to premier October 18, 2015. This documentary aired over seven consecutive nights and depicted how people with a wide range of beliefs search for deeper meaning and connection with the world around them, illuminating the best of faith and spiritual practices from around the world—the rituals, stories and relationships that bind us all together as human beings.[2]

To understand what Oprah is working to achieve is to understand what Oprah believes herself. On one occasion, she said, "While

Christianity is a valid way to achieve high states of spirituality, it must not be considered a unique way, or a 'correct way.'"[3] On another occasion, she said, "I'm a free-thinking Christian who believes in my way, but I don't believe it's the only way, with 6 billion people on the planet."[4] In addition to her millions of television followers, Oprah has 31.8 million Twitter followers.[5] How many biblically based Christian leaders and pastors have 38 million Twitter followers? Oprah's spirituality is rooted in an acceptance of religious pluralism, and she is spreading the false belief that all religions lead to the same spiritual truth.

A poll conducted at beliefnet.com found that 33 percent of 6,600 respondents said Oprah has had "a more profound impact" on their spiritual lives than their own clergy.[6] While this notion of religious pluralism is compelling to millions of Oprah's fans, and others, this book will show some serious reasons as to why all roads cannot lead to the same spiritual truth. It will proclaim emphatically that all roads do not lead to Heaven.

I was watching television at the YMCA one day when my friend Nancy, who was working out on the machine next to me, looked at the TV screen and said: "What is the big issue with all religions?" It was a small Y, where everybody knew each other. I had befriended Nancy for more than three years. I knew that her grandfather was African-American, her grandmother was Native American, and her husband was into philosophy. I associated Nancy's seemingly deep faith in God with her grandfather who she said grew up in the South as a very committed Christian.

I understood Nancy's worldview to be predominantly Christian, though her grandmother had probably held an animistic view (belief in gods of the rocks and sky) before meeting her husband. Nancy spoke frequently about her faith in Jesus Christ and called herself a strong Christian. On this particular day at the Y, she was indignant that anyone would fail to embrace the belief that all religions, including Islam and Judaism, were vehicles to Heaven. I was taken aback. I asked, "Do you really think that all religions lead to God?" She said, "Absolutely."

Because I knew Nancy's background, I felt both comfortable and obligated to tell her that if she denies that Jesus Christ is the only way to Heaven she is not what the Bible would classify as a Christian. She is not saved by the blood of Christ, who alone died on the cross for our sins. I gently reminded her that these are not my words, but the words of Jesus. In John 14:6, Jesus said, "I am the way and the truth and the life. No one comes to the Father except through me." Nancy became aggressive, but I stood my ground, with love and kindness. Later, I learned that she filed a complaint against me with the Y's corporate managers.

Nancy had accepted the theory of religious pluralism. I was saddened that she never accepted the free gift of salvation in Christ, and that our friendship disintegrated. But I cannot deny the truth of God to accommodate any human being.

A couple of years later, Barna Research and the American Bible Society did a joint study asking people if they believed that all roads lead to Heaven. The study helped to shed light on the topic of religious pluralism, which is the belief that:

1. All roads lead to the same spiritual Truth.
2. Every religion is true.
3. Each religion provides a genuine encounter with the Ultimate.
4. While one may be better than the others, all are adequate truths or ways to Heaven.[7]

Do You Believe That the Bible, the Book of Mormon and the Quran All Lead To The Same Spiritual Truth?

In a 2012 Barna survey, Americans were asked to respond to this statement: "The Bible, the Koran, and the Book of Mormon are all different expressions of the same spiritual truths." Fifteen percent of participants agreed strongly, 31 percent agreed somewhat, 18 percent disagreed somewhat, 28 percent disagreed strongly, and 8 percent were not sure.[8]

Three years later, in the *2015 State of the Bible* survey, Americans were asked to respond to the same statement. Overall, one out of six (16 percent) strongly agreed, only one percentage point below the 2011 response. Thirty-two percent agreed somewhat, 16 percent disagreed somewhat, 28 percent disagreed strongly, and 9 percent were uncertain.[9]

The Bible, the Quran, and the Book of Mormon are all different expressions of the same spiritual truths. *	2011	2012	2013	2014	2015
agree strongly	17	15	16	18	16
agree somewhat	33	31	31	29	32
disagree somewhat	17	18	19	15	16
disagree strongly	28	28	28	29	28
not sure	6	8	7	9	9

American Bible Society State of the Bible 2015, Table 1.2 /— Beliefs about the Bible Page 34 of 79.

The Younger the Generation—The Greater Belief In Religious Pluralism

Of those who strongly agreed with the statement, Millennials polled at 18 percent, Generation Xers at 18 percent, Boomers at 15, and Elders at 11. Protestants strongly agreed to the statement, at 10 percent, Catholics at 15 percent. Nonpracticing faiths calling themselves Christian agreed at 17 percent, and those of other faiths or no faith, 20 percent.[10] With each new generation, we see an increase in the percentage of those who hold to the belief that all religions lead to the same spiritual truth. This is a wakeup call for the church, and it highlights the need for apologetics and good philosophy, both of which would expose a major problem with religious pluralism: It's logically self-defeating, culturally intolerant, and offensive to every culture, worldview, and religion. Given this truth, the younger generation and the church in general would begin to see the truth about religions pluralism.

The Challenge for Religious Pluralism—The Belief that All Roads Lead To Heaven

The *COEXIST* bumper sticker should be changed to *CONTRADICT*. The bumper sticker is a poster child for *Religious Pluralism,* and it proclaims that all religions are equal and lead to the same spiritual truth—Heaven. The problem with the COEXIST belief is that it contradicts itself—it's self-defeating and intolerant. Furthermore, each individual religion rejects this notion as an offense against its own cultural and religious beliefs. Since the inception of time, all religions have coexisted, with the exception of Islam. Religious pluralism is self-defeating because it denies the logical laws called *First Principles* of Logic. For example, let's apply pluralism to the logical *law of identity*. The law of identity states that a thing must be identical to itself or it would not be itself and that a religion must be identical to itself or it would not in fact be itself. Any religion without a unique identity cannot exist as its own religion, because without that unique identity, it would not be. This begs the question; how can religious pluralism exist as an entity without an identity? Nothing can exist without an entity-hence religious pluralism cannot exist. Put another way, if Jesus and Muhammad were the same people, or if Christianity and Islam were the same religion, they would have to look, believe, and proclaim exactly the same. If they look different by their identity, their beliefs, and proclamations, then they do not share the same identity. Hence, they cannot by their own existence and proclamation lead to the same eternal resting place.

To exist is to exist as something, and that means to exist with a particular identity. Christianity exists due to its unique correlation to the truth, traditions, and beliefs.[11] The same can be truth for Judaism, Islam, and Hinduism. To have an identity means to have a single identity and an object or a religion cannot have two identities. A tree cannot be a telephone and Christianity cannot be Islam and Hinduism cannot be Judaism. The claim that all religions ultimately lead to the same spiritual truth still connotes an exclusive claim of a *singular truth,* and this denies the possibility of any plurality of beliefs from its very definition. Logic mandates that there must be one truth and to be *the* truth makes all others definitions of God and paths to God false.

The Barna/American Bible Society survey question only addressed the Bible, the book of Mormon, and the Quran. Had it included the Hindu Vedas or any other religious texts, I am confident they would have concluded with the same forty-six percent believing that all religions lead to the same spiritual truth. In the end, in 2015, 47 percent of Americans polled belied that the Bible, the Quran, and the book of Mormon are all different expressions of the same spiritual truth. Forty-seven percent of American's polled hold to the belief that *all roads lead to Heaven*. Sadly, my friend Nancy, who called herself a Christian, held the same false belief.

With each new generation we are seeing a progression in the belief that all roads lead to the same spiritual truth. While this poses a number of problems, what lies at stake is the eternal destiny of our children and grandchildren. It is for this reason that we should pause to address the all-important eternal question, "Do all roads truly lead to Heaven"?

NOTES:

[1] Muhammad Ali, Edited by David West, *The Mammoth Book of Muhammad Ali,* (Philadelphia, PA: Running Press Book Publishers, 2012), *Biography Online,* http://www.biographyonline.net/sport/quotes/muhammad-ali.html https://www.facebook.com/MuhammadAliVerified/posts/530413613641300.

[2] Oprah Presents Landmark TV Event *Belief* Premiering Sunday, October 18 on OWN, http://www.oprah.com/belief/Oprah-Winfrey-Presents-Landmark-Television-Event-Belief.

[3] Floyd and Mary Beth Brown, "Oprah's Evolution," *Townhall* (March 13, 2008), at http://townhall.com/columnists/floydanmarybethbrown/2008/03/13oprahs_evolution/page/full.

[4] Adelle M. Banks, "Oprah's gospel' influence concerns some Christians," *USA Today* (July 9, 2008), at http://usatoday30.usatoday.com/news/religion/2008-07-07-oprah-christian_N.htm.

[5] https://twitter.com/Oprah?ref_src=twsrc%5Egoogle%7Ctwcamp%5Eserp%7Ctwgr%5Eauthor

[6] Ann Oldenburg, "The divine Miss Winfrey?" *USA Today* (May 11, 2006), at http://usatoday30.usatoday.com/life/people/2006-05-10-oprah_x.htm.

[7] Norman L. Geisler, *Bakers Encyclopedia of Christian Apologetics,* (Grand Rapids, MI: Baker Books, Fourth Printing . June 2000), 598.

[8] American Bible Society, Barna Group, *The State of the Bible 2012,* Table 1.29: Beliefs About The Bible; Data Asked Online And Phone. Research commissioned by: American Bible Society, Research conducted by: Barna Group, 31.

[9] American Bible Society State of the Bible 2015, Table 1.2 /- Beliefs about the Bible. Page 34 of 79.

[10] Beliefs about the Bible [Table 1.2, page 33]. http://www.americanbible.org/uploads/content/State_of_the_Bible_2015_report.pdf

[11] Geisler, *BECA,* 250.

CHAPTER 1

DO ALL RELIGIONS LEAD TO THE SAME SPIRITUAL TRUTH?

To believe in God is to yearn for His existence and, furthermore, it is to act as if He did exist. —Miguel de Unamuno[1]

"Six Blind Men and an Elephant"

In this well-known Indian fable, six blind men go out into the jungle to visit an elephant that's quietly basking in the summer sun. Each man is told to reach out and touch the object directly in front of him. When they were asked what they believed they were touching, the men responded as follows: The first man touched the elephant's trunk and thought it was a snake. The man who touched the elephant's tusk said it was a spear. The man who touched the elephant's leg said it was a tree trunk. The man who touched the tail said it was a rope. The man who touched the side of the elephant believed it was a wall; and, finally, the man who touched the elephant's ear said it was a fan.

The men were arguing about which answer was correct when a wise man stopped by and calmly explained: "All of you are right. The reason each of you is telling it differently is because each one of you touched a different part of the elephant. The elephant has all the features that all of you said."

This story illustrates the concept of *Religious Pluralism,* which is "the belief that every religion is true and that each provides a genuine encounter with the Ultimate. While one may be better than the other, all religions are adequate."[2] Thus, in this view, all religions hold truth, even if this truth is only partially correct, just as the six blind men were only partially correct. And all religions provide the way to the desired eternal state. No one religion, then—not Judaism, Hinduism, Islam, Christianity, Taoism, nor Buddhism—can claim to be exclusively true.[3]

But what if the blind men could suddenly see? Would their perspective of the elephant become clearer? Many of us tend to be willfully blind. We don't want to be convicted by the truth about God. If we can remain blind to God's existence, we can ignore the truth about God's existence, and we don't have to believe in Jesus.[4]

Consider the story of the man who had been blind in John 9. Note his sudden transformation: "They brought to the Pharisees the man who had formerly been blind. Now it was a Sabbath day when Jesus made the mud and opened his eyes. So the Pharisees again asked him how he had received his sight. And he said to them, 'He put mud on my eyes, and I washed, and I see'" (John 9:13-15, ESV). This man was clearly elated that he could see; yet many of us don't want our eyes opened. In the biblical story, the Pharisees didn't want to believe Jesus' miraculous sign that He was God. They kept asking the blind man how he was able to see because they didn't want to believe it: "A second time they summoned the man who had been blind. 'Give glory to God by telling the truth,' they said. 'We know this man is a sinner.' He [the blind man] replied, 'Whether he [Jesus] is a sinner or not, I don't know. One thing I do know. I was blind but now I see!'" (John 9:24-25). If the six blind men could see as the man Jesus healed was able to see, they would see the elephant and realize there is a vast difference between their own blind understanding and the knowledge of the truth.

Can All Religions Coexist?

Of course they can! Haven't they done so for thousands of years? And sometimes they even coexist peacefully. But if one subscribes to the notion that all religions are equal, and there is no single theistic God to set rules and boundaries, then man becomes the measure of all things. And if we make man the measure of all things, we would suddenly all be at war because the only thing keeping man from conquering other men is the ultimate standard for goodness found in almighty God.

Since the tragedy of 9/11, the belief in pluralism has become more widespread. Of all the religions represented in the popular *COEXIST* bumper sticker, it seems extreme Islam is the one creating the most disharmony. Since 9/11, Islam has created a disdain for all things religious, namely Christianity. The terrorist attacks generated two negative responses: people either hate all things religious or they believe that all religions lead to Heaven.

The events of 9/11 have led to a more vocal atheism in our nation. The New Age thinking of many nominal Christians, combined with the rise of atheism, has helped spread the belief that religion is the cause of all social strife, and that if we could just be our own gods, we could somehow get along and live peacefully as one happy family. Nothing could be further from the truth, and for those who disagree, they just need to look at other governments around the world and ask themselves, "Are people treated better in other countries than here in America, where Judeo-Christian principles and values have been our bedrock?" If you were born in this country, and you have never had the privilege to go on a Christian mission trip to a less developed country, you may want to consider making that your next vacation. Better yet, consider staying in a country under strong socialist or communist rule. I promise that anyone who experiences life firsthand in one of these countries will then view the Judeo-Christian principles and values of American society as second to none.

The Bible instructs us in Matthew 5:39 to turn the other cheek when we are under attack. But we have turned our entire head, and we've turned it way too far due to the intense pressure from the political correctness movement and the misguided inter-faith movement. As a result, we are now facing the New Age Movement (NAM), which is society's attempt to make Jesus into a religiously pluralistic leader rather than the Son of God.

Questions For Reflection And Discussion
1. What is religious pluralism?
2. What does the six blindfolded men and the elephant represent?
3. If religious pluralism includes Jesus Christ as "a way," does that make it true?
4. What is the significance of the Barna Research study?
5. What general percentage of Americans believe that the Bible, Koran, and Book of Mormon all lead to the same spiritual truth?
6. What do you think the phrase spiritual truth means?

NOTES:

[1] Miguel de Unamuno—*The Tragic Sense of Life*, 8.

[2] Norman L. Geisler, *Baker Encyclopedia of Christian Apologetics*, (Grand Rapids, Mich.: Baker Books, 2000), 598.

[3] Geisler, *BECA*, 598.

[4] Geisler, *Pluralism*, PowerPoint classroom presentation, copyright, 2005, Slide 6.

CHAPTER 2

IS THE JESUS OF THE NEW AGE MOVEMENT THE SAME AS THE JESUS OF THE BIBLE?

"God created man in his own image, says the Bible, and the philoso-phers do just the opposite—they create God in theirs." —George Lichtenberg,[1]

"Some years ago a South American company purchased a fine printing press from a firm in the United States. After it had been shipped and completely assembled, the workmen could not get it to operate properly. The most knowledgeable personnel tried to remedy the difficulty and bring it into proper adjustment, but to no avail. Finally, the company wired a message to the manufacturer, asking them to send a representative immediately to fix it. Sensing the urgency of the request, the U.S. firm chose the person who had designed the press. When he arrived on the scene, the South American officials were skeptical because he was a young man. After some discussion, they sent this cable to the manufacturer: "Your man is too young; send more experienced person." The reply came back: "He made the machine. Let him fix it!"[2]

Scripture tells us in Genesis 1: "Then God said, 'Let us make mankind in our image, in our likeness, so that they may rule over the fish in the sea and the birds in the sky, over the livestock and all the wild animals, and over all the creatures that move along the ground.' So God created mankind in his own image, in the image of God he created them; male and female he created them" (Genesis 1:26-27). When God used the pronoun *us* in verse 26, He was speaking of the Father, the Son Jesus Christ, and the Holy Spirit. We were made in the image of God, in the image of Jesus Christ. Like the men who had no confidence in the young man who created the printing press, we as God's created creatures tend to lack confidence in Him as the true Creator of the universe. Instead, we tend to ask for something other than the Original Creator to guide us through and fix our often self-inflicted errors in life. But like the printing press, we have a problem: since the beginning of time, we have repeatedly tried to make God in *our* image. And like the printer that needed its creator to fix it, we need our Creator God to restore us to the purpose He has for us."

The logical progression for those who deny the deity of Jesus Christ and His unique nature is evolutionary godhood, which leads each individual to the false belief that he or she is a finite "god." This is made very clear in what has become the largest misconception of God in our culture—the New Age Movement.

The New Age Movement is really Hinduism with a modern, westernized, and more materialistic twist. The one distinct difference between Hinduism and the New Age Movement is the fact that while Hinduism is world *denying*, the New Age Movement is world *affirming*.[3] Hinduism was born out of India, during a time of classicism, discomfort, and the lack of material comfort and amenities. Hinduism is a religion of works, which believes that all is not as it seems, and that one is continuously reincarnated until he comes back at a higher level, at which time he is able to realize that all is not real. It is when one has achieved this realization that he becomes part of the oneness; all is one and one is all. This philosophy grew out of a combination of worldviews called *monism* and *pantheism*. Pantheism is the worldview that believes that God is the All or God is the Universe. Pantheism says God *is everything that is*. Examples include Hinduism and Buddhism. Monism sees all as "one." God and the universe are one thing. Christianity holds that God differs from creation.[4]

The New Age folks have taken the best of Hinduism, which is the ability to keep coming back for another life (reincarnation); and relativism, the lack of any standard of right from wrong, and added a modern, twenty-first century context to the framework of the Hindu religion. For example, people all over America refer to "karma" as positive or negative destiny when in correct context it refers to cause and effect. This is quite opposite from Hinduism's concept of Karma that's found in India. If you or I touch a hot stove, we will burn our hand. That is karma understood in its correct context. Furthermore, in the context of Hinduism, karma directly relates to one's being good and doing good in an effort to reach the next level of reincarnation. If you are good, you move up to a rabbit or a bear. If you are bad, you might slide down to a roach.

In America, reincarnation is always directly related to past royalty or some other great heritage. When was the last time you heard a Hollywood star say they descended from a reincarnated roach or dung-eating beetle? The New Age Movement makes everything better through relative thinking because if all is relative then truth becomes whatever you want it to be—at least in theory.

For NAM, absolute truth is traded in for relativism, which flows out of the Yin and Yang. Yen and yang refers to the balance of all things as opposed to absolute to one side or the other.[5] The New Age movement takes this major religious system of Hinduism and adds to it the affluence and modern comforts of a post-modern and enlightened world. This addition quickly alters the path of traditional Hinduism and seeks new direction. For what modern day professional is going to abandon all of their material, worldly possessions to go meditate under a tree? This would be *self-denying*. Instead, they get into their materialistic SUV or their *green* hybrid vehicle with air conditioning and digital radios and go to Yoga class for *self-affirmation* in order to feel better. What New Age person ever said they were afraid of coming back in their next life as a termite or a roach?

The New Age Movement includes many beliefs, ranging from Wicca, Witchcraft, Neo-Hinduism, to nominal Christianity. If truth is relative, then all roads can in theory lead to the same spiritual truth. The greatest threat to orthodox Christianity is relative beliefs and application to Christian Scripture. One of the most visible examples of this is in the New Age Movement and "positive thinking, which seeks to enact control of the adherents' external being or life through their own power.

New Age writer Lord Maitreya is considered by some to be the New Age Christ. Maitreya teaches that one ought not to fear because all of Light and Truth lies within each heart, and man will become God once he realizes this.[6] The difference between the New Age Christ and the biblical Christ is that the biblical Christ proves to be authentic by his uniqueness. By denying that Christ is unique, NAM reduces Him to the level of other gods. If Jesus Christ is merely one among all other gods, then Christianity and the Bible become equal among all other religions, and God is considered relative.

NAM Claims That Jesus Is Not Unique

If Jesus Christ is not unique, then He is the same as all other finite humans that have ever walked the earth. This makes it easier to justify man as a god. According to NAM, all men have innate divinity with the potential to become Christ(s). All men are divine in the same way that Christ is divine. NAM says that although Christ was the most advanced human being ever to walk Planet Earth, He is not God. He is merely a divine being. Furthermore, NAM believes that Jesus Christ and Lucifer are of the same and equal force and are simply moving in opposite directions. David Spangler, author of the New Age book *Reflections on the Christ,* wrote: "Christ is the same force as Lucifer but moving in a seemingly opposite direction. Lucifer moves in to create the light within, through the pressure of experience. Christ moves out to release that light, that wisdom, that love into creation ..." [7]

The Yin and Yang principle mandates a balance between the two. If uniqueness were given to Jesus Christ, there would be sin in the sense of creating an *imbalance* between Jesus and Lucifer, or *good* and *evil*.

The ultimate purpose and end goal of NAM is to prevent light, love, and wisdom from stagnating and to release these attributes, which have been forged in the furnace of creation, to become an illumination onto the world.[8]

The Biblical Response to NAM's Claims That Jesus Christ Is Not Unique

The Bible is very clear about who Jesus Christ is and what He taught. The biblical person of Jesus Christ is very different from, and in direct contrast to, the person of Jesus Christ portrayed by NAM. Scripture is clear that Jesus is unique in nature as the only incarnation of God (John 1:1, 14) as well as the one and only Savior of the world (John 3:16, 18; Phil. 2:1-8; 1 John 2:2).[9] Jesus was more than just a mortal man as NAM portrays. Jesus Christ is not just Jesus who attained Christhood in the same way NAM claims that others can achieve Christhood. Christ proclaimed His uniqueness in what He said: "I am the bread of life. He who comes to me will never go hungry, and whoever believes in me will never be thirsty" (John 6:35). Jesus also said that while He is in the world, He is the light of the world (John 9:5). He said He is the gate through which one can be saved for eternity (John 10:9). Finally, Jesus proclaimed that He and God the Father are one (John 10:30). Other supportive Scriptures include John 11:25 and John 14:6. It is crucial to one's salvation to understand who the real Christ is. Faith in a counterfeit Christ will lead to a counterfeit salvation.[10]

While religious pluralism in the form of the New Age Movement offers a counterfeit faith, an essential component necessary for us to respond to the COEXIST proclamation that all roads lead to Heaven is to understand worldviews. Once we understand what the different worldviews are, we will be better equipped to understand how to answer with the Truth of Jesus Christ in light of the New Age Movement, Islam, and the progressive politically correct culture.

Questions For Reflection And Discussion

1. What does NAM stand for?
2. What are five specific hallmarks of the New Age Movement?
3. Where does the Jesus of NAM live and how old is he?
4. What are some of the beliefs that NAM draws from?
5. What is the primary world religion that NAM is based on?
6. Why do you think NAM denies the uniqueness of Jesus?

NOTES:

[1] Bob Phillips, *Phillips Treasury of Humorous Quotations*, (Wheaton, IL: Tyndale House Publishers, Inc., 2004), 109.

[2] Roy B. Zuck, *The Speaker's Quote Book*, Three Minutes A Day (Grand Rapids, MI: Kregel Publications, 1997), 91.

[3] Martin, 330.

[4] Norman Geisler, *Bakers Encyclopedia of Christian Apologetics*. (Grand Rapids, Mich.: Baker Book House, 1999), 495.

[5] Winfried Corduan, *Neighboring Faiths*. (Downers Grove: InterVarsity Press, 1998), 282.

[6] Yutaka J. Amano and Norman L. Geisler, *The Infiltration of the New Age*, (Wheaton, Ill.: Tyndale House Publishers, Inc., 1989), 18.

[7] David Spangler, *Reflections of the Christ,* (Findhorn, Scotland: Findhorn, 1978), 40.

[8] Amano and Geisler, *The Infiltration of the New Age*, 116.

[9] Amano and Geisler, *The Infiltration of the New Age*, 125.

[10] Ron Rhodes, *The Counterfeit Christ of The New Age Movement*, (Grand Rapids, Mich.: Baker Book House, 1990), 168.

CHAPTER 3

WILL HOW WE SEE GOD DETERMINE HOW WE SEE THE WORLD?

"Various forms of religious madness are quite common in the United States."[1] —Alexis de Tocqueville

Early in December of 2015, one week after the San Bernardino, California, terrorist attack that killed 14 people and injured 22, my mobile phone rang. It was my wife calling me from outside of our house. I was inside, in our home office. She told me in a concerned voice that the home contractor company representative had arrived as scheduled. His name was Muhammad, and he had a large Bowie knife. I calmly went out to meet Muhammad regarding access to our crawl space, and the first thing I asked myself was, "Should I not give this person who looks like a Muslim, has the name Muhammad, and is carrying a very large Bowie knife a reason for the truth and hope that we as Christians have?" (1 Peter 3:15).

I wondered how Muhammad viewed the world. As a Muslim, he was almost certain to subscribe to the theory of absolute truth. *Metaphysical Relativism* proclaims that there are no absolutes anywhere in reality, and *Epistemological Relativism* proclaims there are no absolutes in human knowledge—that knowledge in relation to truth is relative to things such as time, space, culture, society, and history. I surmised that Muhammad didn't embrace any category of relativism because while the Islamic faith is wrong about who God is, it is right about moral absolutes and absolute truth. My starting point for sharing Christ with someone like who I perceived Muhammad to be would be to reason from absolute truth, that a theistic God of the universe exists—then I would make my way to the fact that Jesus Christ *is* Truth. If Muhammad was an atheist or agnostic, I would have to start by addressing the belief that truth is relative, which would render the existence of God and the person of Jesus Christ as the true God relative. I decided that I would approach Muhammad by addressing what truth *is*.

First, *truth is what corresponds to reality.* This includes the fact that truth is *transcultural.* By this I mean that 2+2=4, for all people, in all cultures, at all times. I was born in America, the son of a Sicilian immigrant and raised in Western culture according to the Christian faith and absolute truth. Muhammad, from his accent, was probably born in India, where the philosophical and theological position about truth is relative. However, as a Muslim, Muhammad would surely reject relativism. I saw this potential conflict as a good starting point for sharing the Truth of Jesus Christ with him. If I could get Muhammad to reason for truth, then I could show him logically that just as 2+2=4 for Muslims, Hindus, and Christians, it is also true that Jesus Christ as the Son of God *is* God and not just a prophet. This would create a starting point for me to share the truth that Jesus is the true God.

Second, *truth is telling it as it really is.* In John 18:38, Pilate asked Jesus, "What is truth?" This indicates that Pilate knew some truth. Furthermore, by telling the screaming mob that he could find no fault in Jesus, Pilate was telling it like it was. In the politically correct world that we find ourselves today, telling it like it really is has become intolerance—in the name of tolerance.[2] The truth is that political correctness is hypocritical, self-defeating, and unable to always withstand the truth. Truth levels the playing field in that God asks us to use fair and balanced scales. "Honest scales and balances belong to the Lord; all the weights in the bag are of his making" (Proverbs 16:11). Furthermore, "The Lord detests differing weights, and dishonest scales do not please him" (Proverbs 20:23). While the Lord is using the weighing of metals as currency, the principle He is speaking to is honesty, in all of life's transactions—including how we speak and our use of words. Political correctness is man's effort to control the meaning of words and truth. Political correctness is at odds with truth because *telling it as it is* means speaking the truth, including the truth about God.

Truth is what is. The earth is round, not flat. Jesus Christ is the Son of God, not just a prophet, or a great religious and moral man. *First Principles of Logic*—the simple logical essentials behind the process by which we discover all things about and in the world—affirms this.[3] A First Principle, the *Law of Noncontradiction,* says that op-posite ideas cannot be true and not true at the same time and in the same sense. This means that Islam and Christianity cannot both be truth at the same time and in the same sense. The same can be said of Christianity and Hinduism, which simply means, "the religion of India."[4] The Medieval Muslim philosopher Avicenna said, "Anyone who denies the *Law of Noncontradiction* should be beaten and burned until he admits that to be beaten is not the same as to not be beaten, and to be burned is not the same as to not be burned!"[5] The *First Principles of Logic* tells it like it is. These principles are tools that we use to discover all other truths. Without them we couldn't learn anything else. By not telling the truth, or not saying it like it is, we become confused about knowing anything absolutely and for certain. This seemed like a good starting point for me to begin conversing with Muhammad.

In giving a reason for truth, I could proclaim that truth can be known, which in turn leads to the conclusion that the truth about God can be known. If truth can be known then we can absolutely know which god is the true God. By exposing the truth about the absolute truth, we clear the way to the absolute existence of the true God of the universe. This is the mission of my ministry, Reason for Truth—to enable believers to use apologetics in evangelism.

While I was greeting our home inspector Muhammad, my mobile phone rang. A friend had called to encourage me and let me know that he is praying for my ministry. I thanked him for praying for us and let that conversation be heard by Muhammad as a precursor to my asking him about his cultural and religious beliefs. As I got to know a little bit about Muhammad, I learned that he was indeed from India and that he and his family grew up in the Islamic faith. As it turns out, he carries the Bowie knife because he runs into snakes and varmints when working under residential crawl spaces.

Since coming to America, he, his mother, and his two brothers had all gotten saved! In fact, they were attending a local church pastored by a dear friend of mine who ministers to a multicultural community. I was no longer in doubt of his worldview. As we talked, I could see the love of God—of Jesus Christ—in him. As I went back inside my home, it occurred to me that we never know who we are speaking with. I was thankful to learn that Muhammad was a believer in Jesus Christ, but I was reminded again how we must *always* be *ready* and *willing* to give a reason for the truth and the hope that lies within us as believers in Jesus Christ, even when it might seem uncomfortable or politically incorrect. Understanding worldviews is essential to our being able to perceive how other people understand the world around them, the universe, and most important, how they understand God.

What Is a Worldview?

A worldview is a mental model of reality—a framework of ideas and attitudes about the world, ourselves, and life; a comprehensive system of beliefs with answers to a wide range of life's questions such as, what are humans, why are we here, and what is our purpose?[26] All worldviews lead back to questions about God: Can we know God exists? Have miracles occurred in the past, as claimed by the Bible, and do they occur in the present? Does God communicate with us, and if so, how? What happens to us after death?

Theologian and Philosopher Dr. Norman Geisler describes world-view as an interpretive framework through which or by which we make sense out of the data of life. It is how we view or interpret reality. If God and the universe exist, then either there is one God or many gods. If there are many gods, then the polytheistic worldview is correct. If there is only one God, then this God is either finite or infinite. If there is one finite god, then finite *godism* is correct. If this finite god has two poles, one being beyond and one in the world, then *panentheism* (god is in all) is right. If there is one infinite God, as Judaism, Christianity, and Islam believe, then God either intervenes in the world and the universe or He does not. If there is intervention, then *theism* (God created all) is true. If God does not intervene in the world and universe, then *deism* (God created all but does not intervene) is true.[7]

It is through our worldview that we determine our priorities, our relationship with God, and our relationship with our fellow human beings. Our worldview instructs and directs our entire life, answering questions like a road map that provides direction and guidance.

Everyone Has a Worldview

A worldview is like a set of glasses that determines or taints our vision of God, objectivity, and morality. Our worldview is formed through our educational experience, our family upbringing, the culture we live in, the books we read, and the influence of the media we subscribe to. Most of us have never given great thought to what we believe. We are unable in many cases to state a rational defense and reason for our beliefs. The Christian worldview is theistic and believes that God exists

(Heb. 11:6), and that man is not the measure of all things, but that God is the measure of all things. God created all of us and everything that exists (Gen. 1:1), and Jesus holds everything together (Col. 1:17).

Theologian A.W. Tozer made this observation: "Were we able to extract from any man a complete answer to the question, 'What comes into your mind when you think about God?' we might predict with certainty the spiritual future of that man."[8] Tozer was saying in part that an individual's understanding of the nature of God ultimately affects their worldview, which in turn determines what they believe about morality and how they live out that morality. Each worldview understands God differently and holds to a view that is equally exclusive and narrow. Each worldview is incompatible with all of the other worldviews because of its differing claims about God.

An examination of the evidence begs the question: "What makes a non-Christian worldview deceptive?" A deceptive worldview is one in which Satan tries to con us into thinking a certain set of beliefs is absolute truth, when in reality it is not. A deceptive worldview is just that. It's deceptive. While it looks like the truth on the surface, it is far from it. In our next chapter we will look at the three main worldviews and how they affect different culture.

Questions For Reflection And Discussion

1. What is a worldview?
2. List three good ways to describe truth?
3. Does everyone have a worldview—and what is yours?
4. What is meant by having a Christian worldview?
5. What is determined or guided by our worldview?

NOTES:

[1] Alexis de Tocqueville, *Democracy in America*, II, II, 2.

[2] Steven Garofalo, *Right For You, But Not For Me—A Response To Moral Relativism*, (Charlotte, N.C.: Triedstone Publishing Company, 2013), 253.

[3] IBID., 202.

[4] Winfried Corduan, *A Christian Introduction to World Religions Neighboring Faiths*, Downers Grove, Ill.: InterVarsity Press, 1998), 189.

[5] Norman L. Geisler, *I Don't Have Enough Faith to Be an Atheist*, (Wheaton, Ill: Crossway Books, 2004), 57.

[6] *What Is A Worldview?* The American Scientific Affiliation, http://asa3.org/ASA/education/views/index.html.

[7] Geisler, BECA, 786-787.

[8] A.W. Tozer, *The Knowledge of the Holy*, (New York, N.Y.: HarperSanFrancisco, 1961), 1.

CHAPTER 4

WHAT ARE THE MAJOR WORLDVIEWS IN RELATION TO MAJOR WORLD RELIGIONS?

"Christians should be a foreign influence, a minority group in a pagan world."[1] —Billy Graham

In this chapter we will define and evaluate the three major worldviews and show why they cannot all be true. Scripture warns us to not be taken captive by the deceptive philosophies and worldviews spreading throughout our culture (Col. 2:8).

Judaism, Christianity, and Islam are the three major *theistic* religions in the world, and they fall under the Theism worldview. All other worldviews are non-theistic. As part of defining our terms, we have provided a brief explanation of each of the major worldviews. These worldviews are no longer found only in faraway countries; they are now prevalent in communities, doctor's offices, gas stations, and office cubicles all across the United States.

1. **PANTHEISM: God Is All** (Includes Zen Buddhism, Hinduism, and New Age).
2. **ATHEISM: No God At All** (Includes Buddhism, Taoism, and Religious Humanism).
3. **THEISM: God Made All** (Includes Judaism, Christianity, and Islam).

Atheism and Theism are mutually exclusive worldviews. Because each holds to certain narrow beliefs, it is logically impossible to also hold a contrasting worldview. To make such a claim would be self-contradicting and, in turn, self-defeating.[2] For example, while atheism holds to the belief that there is no God at all, theism believes in only one, supernatural God. These two views are obviously incompatible because they contradict one another, and both cannot be right. While Pantheism is not mutually exclusive in believing that all roads lead to Heaven, its model is just as mutually exclusive as theism and atheism because it carries its own unique truth claim that "all is God." While Pantheism is mutually exclusive regarding all religions as equal vehicles to God and Heaven, its explanation of the nature of God is completely different from both atheism and theism. Pantheism holds that all religions (as one category) must be included as vehicles to the same spiritual truth. This is just as exclusive as theism and atheism by its very nature.

The Basic Worldviews Described

1) Pantheism. God is the All or God is the Universe. Pantheism is the view that God *is everything that is.* Pantheism identifies the universe

with God. English deist John Toland (1670-1722) first used the term
pantheism in 1705 when he taught that "God is the mind of the soul
of the universe." The problem with Pantheism is that it fails to distinguish the Creator from the created, a distinction made clear in the
very first verse of the Bible.[3] Hinduism and Buddhism are examples
of Pantheism. Some years back, I visited a church in Hawaii and asked
the pastor what were some of the more common theological issues he
faced on the island. He told me that one day after trimming the hedges
in front of their building, he came outside to find a young man walk-
ing up and down the freshly trimmed hedge line gently petting the
bushes and apologizing to the bushes for the fact that the landscaper
did not really know what he was doing. This young man held to a
pantheistic worldview, which led him to believe that the hedged plants
were literally God since God is all, and as a result, the landscaper had
just trimmed God.

SCIENTIFICALLYY SPEAKING: For the Pantheist there
is no Creator beyond the universe. The Creator and creation
are two different ways of viewing one reality. To the Pantheist,
God is the universe (or the All) and the universe is God. In
Pantheism, God is seen as an *impersonal being* embodied in
the oneness of the universe, so it can be said that God exists
within the entirety of all mankind. The uncaused Cause of
Theism is not the God of Pantheism. Pantheism affirms that an
unlimited and necessary being exists but denies the reality of
limited and finite beings.[4] Pantheism is one of the main worldviews that adheres to relativism because it holds to the belief
that *good* and *evil* are considered illusions and are not real.
Because good and evil are illusions, reality becomes unknown,
and not even history can be said to be real. If Pantheists were

to admit that history does exist, at best it's cyclical as depicted in reincarnation.

Pantheism holds to the belief that miracles are not possible in the sense that they are caused by something outside of the world because there is no all-powerful God outside of the universe. Regarding salvation, Pantheism believes that our destiny is merely the end goal of uniting with the *unknown impersonal God* accomplished through the cycle(s) of reincarnation. It is through reincarnation that one strives to reach nirvana or enlightenment, where they finally discover that their existence as an individual being is not real.[5]

2) Atheism. No God exists in or beyond the universe. Simply put, Atheism denies that any God exists anywhere.

SCIENTIFICALLY SPEAKING: Atheism holds that the universe is eternal. Most secular scientists hold to the belief that the universe came into existence in one moment, that the *Second Law of Thermodynamics*—the belief that the amount of usable energy in the universe is decreasing[6]—scientifically proves that all matter and energy is running down and is not self-perpetuating. The problem for Atheism is that if the universe is disconnected from God and all matter and energy is running down, then the universe cannot be *eternal*. This is very different from the theistic Christian worldview, which believes that the world was created by God out of nothing (*ex nihilo*), that it is growing old, expending its energy, and winding down in the time-space continuum. Atheism holds the exact opposite view, that despite the law of physics and

Albert Einstein's *Theory of General Relativity*, the world is *not* winding down. Their denial is based on the belief that the world and the entire universe were not wound up in creation by an *ultimate Creator*, but self-created by random chance by some form of self-perpetuating energy.

The one thing that the Atheist still cannot answer is where that energy came from. Atheists believe that the universe was uncaused. To admit to a causal existence is to admit to an Ultimate Eternal Causer or better yet a superior being that caused the universe to come into existence. One of the biggest problems that Atheism faces is that science and logic claim that everything and anything that has been created must have a creator. To deny this notion is to deny logic and the laws of physics. Furthermore, the creator must be bigger than the creation. Is the automaker or the watchmaker or the maker of the space shuttle greater than the items they created?

Atheists also deny that miracles are possible and that mankind is made in the image of God (Gen. 1:26). They believe that man is a product of random evolutionary chance and processes, which ultimately denies any possibility of life after death. The most extreme form of Atheism is found in Marxist Communism and by the current Maoist Communist philosophy in China. China has schooled over a billion people in the principles of Atheism, and most of the country of China operates under the assumption that God does not exist.

A form of Atheism prevalent in the United States is *secular humanism*. Secular humanism focuses on the values and interests of human beings. Secular humanism proclaims that man is the measure of all things. Its values are focused on human versus God.[7]

3) Theism. Theism is the worldview that an infinite, personal God created the universe and miraculously intervenes in it from time to time. God is both transcendent over the universe and immanent in it. The three great theistic religions are Judaism, Islam, and Christianity.

Theists can be distinguished by what they believe about God and His relation to the world. Most believe the material world is real, but some believe it exists only in mind and ideas. Most Theists believe that God is unchangeable, but some (generally influenced by Pantheism) believe God can and does change. Some Theists believe it is possible that the created universe is eternal, while most believe the universe must be temporal. Many Theists believe that miracles are possible. Although God operates his universe in a regular and orderly way by the laws of nature, nevertheless, God transcends those laws.

Nature is not the whole story. There is a supernatural realm. This supernatural realm can invade the natural realm. The sovereign Creator cannot be locked outside his creation. Although God normally works in a regular way, on occasion He directly intervenes. This occasional invasion of nature by the supernatural is called a "miracle." Perhaps the most important difference among Theists is that some, mostly those in the Judaism and Islam religions, believe in monotheism, the belief that God is only one person. Others, notably orthodox Christians, believe in a *Trinitarian* form of monotheism: God has three centers of personhood within one perfect mon-theistic unity.[8] These three centers of personhood include God; His Son, Jesus Christ; and the Holy Spirit.

Theism holds that the physical universe is not all that is out there, that there is an infinite, personal God beyond the universe. Furthermore, this personal, infinite God created the universe, sustains it, and holds it all together. This theistic God sometimes supernaturally intervenes in the world. The Bible makes this assertion: "And he is before all things, and in him all things hold together" (Col. 1:17, ESV). In fact, this theistic God will resurrect the dead, and persons will live an immortal and embodied life in the hereafter. This is the traditional view as represented by traditional Judaism, Christianity, and Islam.[9]

The Importance of Worldview

One's worldview is what influences and determines *personal meaning* in life, including moral values. One of the most important questions demanded by each worldview is "Where did we come from?" This determines whether our morality is based on an absolute good God, or on each person's preference, tastes, and desires. Based on these two choices, all moral questions are answered. For example, should we pull the plug on a severely ill patient in a hospital bed? How do we treat or punish criminals? Our answers to these moral questions stem directly from our worldview.

Pantheism's worldview says that we emanated from God like sunrays from the sun or sparks popping out of a campfire. As a result, Pantheists believe that creation is *out of God* Himself (*Ex Deo*). For the Pantheist, death is nothing more than a cessation of one's life, which leads to the next life through reincarnation. The ultimate goal of Pantheism is to work our way up through millions of years of reincarnation and countless life forms to the point that we are finally merged with God, becoming part of the "Oneness" with all others who have reached nirvana or enlightenment. This Oneness holds no real personal relationship with God but holds that each person simply merges into the Oneness of God in the form of *Brahman* or *Nirvana*.[10]

Atheism denies the existence of God. It holds to the belief that all of creation came out of existing matter *(ex-materia)*.[11] More simply, Atheism believes that a bunch of "space junk" came together over millions of years to form the universe, planets, and the earth. But in the end, the Atheist still cannot answer one simple question: "Where did the space junk come from?" And who made the space junk? The Jewish Torah answers this question decisively: "In the beginning God created the heavens and the earth" (Gen. 1:1).

Christians and Jews are *theists.* They believe that God created the universe out of nothing, *ex nihilo.* Biblical theists believe that God created the human race, meaning you and me, with a purpose, and that purpose included the notion that we would fellowship for eternity with Him. This is quite the opposite of Pantheists, who believe that we lose all individual identity in God as we merge up into "Oneness" as a part of the whole, like a spoke in a wheel merges into the hub. Atheists see immortality as a carrying on of the human race through species. Humans live on only in the memory of others for a short period of time, with the role of influencing the generations coming after us. Once forgotten, our impact on future generations becomes thinned out and then nonexistent, apart from our DNA, which is passed on through offspring.[12]

Theistic Worldview No. 1 and No. 2: Judaism and Christianity

Judaism and Christianity fit together like a puzzle, completing one another through the Jewish Torah, Old Testament prophecy, and Christian fulfillment of that prophecy in the New Testament Scriptures. The New Testament cannot be rejected; upon reading both Testaments, it becomes evident that both are necessary to tell the full story of God's creation and involvement in the world and His people. The Torah and Old Testament point to more than 100 prophecies that are fulfilled in the New Testament.

Theistic Worldview No. 3: Islam

Islam's holy book, the Quran, which means to "recite," claims to be the word-for-word verbally inspired Word of God. It is considered to be authoritative, final, and complete— transmitted to the prophet Muhammad by the angel Gabriel over a period of 23 years. Islam's second set of holy writings is the Hadith (traditions), which are an account of what the Prophet said or did. The Hadith was handed down orally for generations. Many of the traditions are transcribed into sharia (Islamic Law), and are the foundation of Islamic law and government. Islamic law and government are based on the *Quran* and the *Hadith*, *Irma* (consensus of the community) and *Quays* (deduction of new rules).

The Quran is more peaceful toward Judaism and Christianity in its early Suras, or chapters, than in later ones. For example, it states that there is no compulsion in religion (Sura 2:256), that Jews and Christians are to obey the Bible (Sura 5:68), and that Muhammad even said to consult Christians for truth (Sura 10:94). But the later Suras speak more negatively toward Jews and Christians. For example, these Suras command its followers to strike off the heads and fingertips of infidels (Sura 8:12), fight them until they are all Muslims (Sura 8:40), strike terror in the hearts of all nonbelievers (Sura 8:60), and make war against unbelievers (Sura 9:29). The Quran also requests Allah to destroy Jews and Christians (Sura 9:30). Not all Muslims hold these views.

Although Muslims claim Muhammad is greater than Jesus, a close examination of both the Christian and Muslim faiths reveals quite the opposite. When comparing the basic beliefs of Muhammad (Islam) to the basic beliefs of Jesus Christ (Christianity) they are one hundred and eighty degrees diametrically opposed. Opposites cannot mean the same thing—and Islam claims that Christianity is not a way to Heaven, and Christianity claims that Islam is not a way to Heaven. Religious pluralism stands on an ideology contrary to each religion, hence fails in its assertion that each religion leads to the same place. Christianity and Islam are so far apart that it renders any notion of pluralistic incorporation impossible. The chart below compares what the New Testament says about Jesus to what the Quran teaches about Muhammad.

MUHAMMAD	JESUS
Not virgin born	Virgin born
Sinful	Sinless
No miracles	Did miracles
Use of sword to advance religion	Forbid sword to advance religion
Retaliated against enemies	Forgave enemies
Motivated by fear	Motivated by love
Overcome by death	Overcame death

Islam is not simply a religion but an inclusive cultural structure that cannot separate religion from the institutions of social provision, government, military, business, and societal behavior. It is theologically impossible for Islam to separate the government and military from organized religion for the simple fact that Islam is a *theocracy* which is a form of government in which God or a deity is recognized as the supreme civil ruler over all society and government authority. Islam is a form of communism based on the Quran and *Sharia Law* as the authority over every area of life. This is a major reason as to why *Islam's theistic worldview* is very different from that of Judaism and Christianity. When people proclaim that the Bible, Quran, and the Book of Mormon all lead to the same spiritual Truth, it begs the question, "What is Truth"? Furthermore, is truth subjective or objective? If truth is *subjective*, then religious pluralism wins the day, but if truth is *objective*, religious pluralism falls flat on its face. For Christians, religious pluralism must be understood as the objective and absolute truth of God or we by default forfeit the theistic-biblical worldview.

> ### Questions For Reflection And Discussion
> 1. What are the main three worldviews?
> 2. What are some religions that fit each of those worldviews?
> 3. What is the importance of one's worldview?
> 4. How does each worldview view Creation?
> 5. What are the only three theistic religions and in what order?
> 6. What are five differences between Islam and Christianity in light of their worldviews and beliefs?

NOTES:

[1] Billy Graham, *Hope for the Troubled Heart* (Dallas: Word, 1991), 43.

[2] Geisler, *BECA*, 786.

[3] Charles C. Ryre, *Basic Theology* (Chicago: Moody Press, 1999), 46.

[4] Norm Geisler, *Systematic Theology In One Volume* (Minneapolis, Minnesota: Bethany House, 2011), 17; 31.

[5] Wayne A. Detzer and Douglas E. Potter, *Cross Cultural Apologetics — Bridging Culture to Defend the Faith,* Copyright 2011 Wayne A. Detzer and Douglas E. Potter, 129-132.

[6] Geisler, *BECA*, 724.

[7] Geisler, 337.

[8] Geisler, *BECA* 722-23.

[9] Geisler, *BECA*, 786.

[10] Geisler, *BECA*, 786.

[11] Geisler, *BECA*, 786.

[12] Geisler, *BECA*, 786.

CHAPTER 5

DOES GOD HAVE A UNIQUE IDENTITY?

"Who is like the Lord our God, the One who sits enthroned on high, who stoops down to look on the heavens and the earth." —King David (Psalm 113:5-6)

Have you ever returned to your car from shopping and put the key in the lock, only to find that it wouldn't turn? You panic as you realize you've gone to the wrong car! The car was the same exact make and color as yours. It was the same year, had the same rims, and was parked in the same row of the parking lot, right next to your car. It was almost identical to your car, but it was not exactly the same. The VIN number was different, it had a different lock, and there was a pinhead-size scratch just above the fender. This is an example of the *Law of Identity*, which says a thing must be identical to itself in order to be itself.

This is true of all things, including the penny in your pocket, you as a person, snowflakes, your fingerprints, and yes—God Himself. If two beings called God were exactly identical, they would not be two separate beings. Likewise, if two religions were exactly the same, they would not exist as two separate bodies of beliefs. Does Hinduism look at all like Christianity or Islam? Does the Book of Mormon, which proclaims many gods, reflect the singular, theistic God of the Bible? They are not remotely close. The fact that each religion has its own unique belief about salvation, Heaven, and who God is leads to the logical conclusion that they are not the same thing because their individual identities are unique.

Can Your Religion Be True for You But Not for Me?

A proponent of religious pluralism might say to a person of a different faith, "Your religion is true for you, but mine is true for me," thus deeming religious truth subjective. But the claim that "religious truth is subjective" assumes that its own view is an objective truth claim! This is hypocritical at best and self-defeating at worst. If even one of those blind men with the elephant had his vision restored to see the truth, then he would look at what he was touching and see that it was an elephant. At that point, wouldn't he be able to show the rest of the men they were wrong by having them feel the whole elephant? The truth is absolute: It was an elephant.

All religions cannot be true because they teach opposite things as truth, and the *Law of Non-Contradiction* states that two systems of religious thought cannot be the same. If they were, they wouldn't be two different religions. As we said already, the *Law of Identity* says an object is the same as itself. If it were not, then it would not be itself. We cannot say, for example, that a tiger, a dog, and an alligator are all elephants. The reason for this is that each animal has its own identity. If all three had the same identity, there would be no differences between them. The same can be said of religion. We cannot say that Christianity, Islam, and Hinduism are all the same because they are all very different and make different truth claims. If all religions led to the same place, it would be mandatory that their core theological doctrines have the same exact identities, and they don't, by any reasonable measure. Pluralism is self-defeating because it fails to keep its identity but melds contradictory identities instead. This point is illustrated below in the simple comparisons of the basic but essential beliefs of Islam and Christianity and between Hinduism and Christianity.[1]

Do you see the vast, unbridgeable differences between the core doctrines of each of these three major world religions? To say that all religions are the same and lead to the same place is to deny any religion its own *unique traditions;* plus it violates the *Law of Identity.* So rather than being tolerant, Pluralism is a very *intolerant* view. Blending all religious beliefs denies each world religion its own unique traditions and doctrines.

ISLAM	CHRISTIANITY
GOD: *Only one person*	**GOD**: Three persons in one God
HUMANITY: *Good by nature*	**HUMANITY**: *Sinful by nature*
JESUS: *Merely a man*	**JESUS**: *More than a man; He was also God*
DEATH OF CHRIST: *He didn't die and rise again*	**DEATH OF CHRIST**: *He died and rose again in the same body*
BIBLE: *Corrupted*	**BIBLE**: *Not corrupted*
SALVATION: *By faith plus works when good deeds outweigh bad ones*	**SALVATION**: *Not by works but is a free gift of God for all who believe*

HINDUISM	CHRISTIANITY
GOD: *There are many gods--Polytheism. God is impersonal; Brahma is an abstract formless eternal being.*	GOD: There is one Theist God--Theism. God is a spiritual being found in three Persons (Matthew 3:13-17; 29:19; 2 Corinthians 13:14).
JESUS CHRIST: *Jesus was one of a number of great holy men (but not perfect). It is an absurd idea that Jesus suffered on the cross. As a holy man, he was beyond pain & suffering.*	JESUS CHRIST: *Jesus is the one and only Son of God. Jesus is above all holy men. Jesus was crucified, suffered and died for our sins on the Cross.*
SIN: *Humanity's problem is "Ignorance."*	SIN: *Humanity is in a state of moral "Rebellion" against God*
SALVATION: *"Enlightenment" brings a man from humanity to God and requires one's personal effort(s).*	SALVATION: *There is only one way to salvation: Through Jesus Christ (John 14:16).*

For example, Islam does not believe that Christ is God and that He died on the cross for the sins of all mankind. Christianity does not believe that Muhammad was a prophet, let alone the last prophet. Hinduism can only accept Jesus as a god among their 300 million other gods, but not the singular "God" of the universe. I would say that Pluralism is politically incorrect and offensive to people in all religions. Looking at all religions is like looking at a bunch of counterfeit twenty dollar bills, trying to find the authentic currency minted by the U.S. government. Only one can be the truth.

Like a Counterfeit Twenty Dollar Bill

What does a counterfeit twenty-dollar bill have in common with a true twenty? Both are on a rectangular piece of paper and both have the number 20 printed on them. If we put a counterfeit beside a true twenty-dollar bill, then the counterfeit becomes obvious in light of the real, true currency. It might be as simple as a shade of ink or a simple dot or line ever so slightly out of place.

How can we tell a counterfeit from the real authentic currency? Not by superficial similarities but by crucial differences—and the same is true of religion. By looking at the crucial differences between religions, we come to the conclusion that all religions cannot be true. Logic mandates that two opposing views cannot both be true. So the concluding question is this: Is there only one way to truth? Christianity answers this question with an emphatic yes. Jesus claimed to be the truth. His disciples affirmed it, and then Jesus proved it. But what about those who say it's true for you, but not for me?

When we speak to what truth is and to the term *Spiritual Truth,* we are speaking to the same thing. The use of these terms begs the question, "What is truth?" Truth can be defined in three simple ways. First, truth is *what corresponds to reality.* Second, truth is *telling it as it is.* Third, truth is what *is.* In each and every case, though, the basis of truth is in God who is the source and standard of righteousness, being, and knowledge.[2] In order for the true God of the universe to be known, we must know the truth about His identity—what differentiates Him from false gods. This leads us to our next chapter, which will address why knowing the truth is so important.

Questions For Reflection And Discussion

1. What does it mean to say that God or a specific religion has a unique identity?
2. Is it possible for one's religion to be true for them but not for someone else?
3. What is the Law of Identity and how does it apply to how we define God and each religion?
4. What is the Law of Non-Contradiction and how does it apply to how we define God and each religion?
5. Why does religious pluralism fail?
6. Do the logical laws of Identity and Non-Contradiction prove that Christianity, Hinduism, Atheism, and Islam cannot all lead to the same spiritual truth?
7. How does the United States Federal Government train to identify counterfeit currency?

NOTES:

---

[1] Geisler, *Pluralism*, slide 40.

[2] BECA 741

CHAPTER 6

WHY IS KNOWING THE TRUTH SO IMPORTANT?

Unless we love the truth we cannot know it.[1] *– Blaise Pascal*

You Must Prove That Hobbits and Neanderthals Don't Exist!

Those were the words texted to me by one of my high school students who had been struggling with her faith in God and her belief in the Bible as the Word of God. This student is a deep thinking young lady who took most of the theology and apologetics classes that I was teaching at our church. There was much more to the discussion, but when she demanded that I prove that Hobbits and Neanderthals don't exist, I had to step back in an effort to see the bigger picture—a rejection of objective truth.

As it turned out, she was watching quite a bit of the National Geographic and Discovery Channel—neither of which is steeped in absolute truth. She sees these and similar networks as experts when it comes to issues such as God, science, and creation. The problem is that while there is truth in much of the programming on these networks, the content they air often promotes non-truths. If you watch closely, you will see that they promote Darwinism and worldviews such as Atheism (no God at all) and Pantheism (all is God). As a result, they project theory as fact and truth. The ability to discern what is true versus a lie is often what we are lacking and where we get led off track. As a result, many of us end up accepting truth as *subjective* instead of *objective*. In turn, our emotional and experiential senses begin to define truth not as objectively rational and logical but subjectively emotional. If truth is knowable and is a referent to reality, we can know that God exists absolutely. Furthermore, we can know which God among all gods is the true God. This is the God that can and will lead us to the road to Heaven. In an effort to understand what truth *is*, I would first like to look at what truth is *not*.

Do You Follow a God or a Religion Because it Works for You?
Truth Is Not What Works—Pragmatism

Hinduism has 33 main Gods, as mentioned in the Hindu sacred writings called the Vedas. However, after the Upanishadic Age, which taught that ultimate reality is a single supreme soul called *Braham* (impersonal, pantheistic form of God)[2], that count went up from 33 gods to over 330 million gods in an attempt to poetically express the infinitude of the universe.[3] Believers in Hinduism can choose to worship one of the 330 million gods of Hinduism, or they can create their own deity and worship it. The idea here is that you choose a god of your liking *that works for you* by hooking up to that venerated deity, like one hooking their cart to a salvific horse of their choosing. In turn, that deity takes you to *Brahman,* which is the Hindu concept of Heaven or afterlife.[4] When we speak of *Brahman*, we must understand that the Hindu concept of Heaven is not like that of the Christian. It is a *oneness* of all things in an impersonal form.

Followers of Hinduism are perfectly accepting of Christians hooking their eternal cart to Jesus as one of the more than 330 million deities leading to Brahman, but they deny Jesus Christ as the *only* way to Heaven or the exclusive theistic God, Creator, and Savior. Do you remember, the Barna/American Bible Societies "State Of The Bible" survey we mentioned in the introduction of this book? It showed that 46 percent of Americans surveyed believe that numerous roads, or religions, lead to the same spiritual truth? This is further evidence that our culture, including many Christians, have accepted the belief that truth is *what works for you*. Truth is not defined or determined by what works for you. The true God—who is the only road to Heaven—is not defined by what works for you or me. Furthermore, truth is not what coheres and the true God is not based on who the populous, governments, or the culture says He is.

Is it True That God Is Who Everyone Says He Is?
Truth Is Not What Coheres

Just because the vast majority of people in India believe in the Hindu faith doesn't make it true that Hinduism is the Truth. Just because the majority of American's identify themselves as Christians does not make Christianity the Truth. The same can be said about Islam in the Middle East. Prior to 630 A.D., the Middle East was predominately Jewish and Christian Polytheistic (belief in many gods). That didn't make Christianity or Judaism the Truth then or Islam the truth now that the Middle East is predominantly Islamic. Truth does not change.

Just because numerous people say the same thing or tell the same story doesn't make what they are saying the truth. Just because the Mormon Church proclaims around the world that Jesus Christ is God doesn't make it true. What the Mormon Church actually teaches is that Jesus is *a god* among many gods. While Mormonism may consider Jesus Christ a little higher than the other gods (Henotheism), the entire church proclaiming that from the hilltops of the world does not make the Mormon's view of Jesus Christ and God the truth. I would submit quite the opposite.

The majority of people in any given culture proclaiming in unison that their idea of God is the truth in and of itself has no bearing on the truth of God. *Consistency* does not define truth.

A set of false statements can be internally consistent. For example, when a group of several witnesses conspire to coherently misrepresent the facts, their testimony becomes coherently false. While their story may cohere, it is still a lie. This is often the strategy in court case scandals involving multiple people. In such cases, defendants collaborate with one another regarding their stories in an effort to gain a new, coherently false story about what the truth is. By doing so, they give the perception that they are all on the same page, speaking the same truth. The end goal in such cases is to create credibility based on the *coherency* of their individual statements as consistent testimony. This is why investigators ask the same questions over and over in an effort to see if there is consistency or inconsistencies within their subject's story. Just because their stories are coherent and consistent does not mean their claim is true. At best, coherence is a negative test of truth.[5] Truth is not what coheres and God is not just who everyone says He is. Furthermore, truth is also not that which was intended. God is not who we intend Him to be.

Is God What One Intends Him to Be?
Truth Is Not That Which Was Intended

In 2008, Connecticut State Attorney General Richard Blumenthal failed to speak the truth when he recalled his military service in Vietnam during a speech he was giving in the election process. Not only did Blumenthal not serve in Vietnam, but he deliberately sought "at least five military deferments from 1965 to 1970 and took repeated steps that enabled him to avoid going to war."[6]

Blumenthal claimed that what he said didn't come out right and that he had proper intentions. Blumenthal may have been sincere in giving this speech, but sincerity doesn't make his statements true. Making a statement that is false does not make the statement true no matter how sincere we may be. Believing that something is true simply because someone intended it to be true would mean that all sincere statements ever uttered were true, even those which were blatantly absurd. It is important for us to understand that even sincere people are often sincerely wrong.[7]

Truth is not what I or anyone else intended to say. When we define truth as what someone else or even we ourselves intended to say, we subscribe to the notion that truth is found in our *intentions* rather than *affirmations*. Just because someone *intends* a statement to be true does not make it true.[8] The same can be said of sincere people with a sincere faith in a false god. The old adage, *the road to hell is paved with good intentions* is fitting for false belief that what was intended is truth. Not only is truth not what was intended, and God's *identity* not determined by who we intend Him to be, but truth is also not what is *comprehensible*. In other words, God is not based on who the secular experts say He is.

Is God Who the Experts Say He Is?

I am amazed by the vast numbers of people who accept most of what they see on television and cable networks. They accept such programs as true because the programs are perceived to be the most comprehensive media source for issues such as science, creation, and religion. Something is not true simply because a group of experts or a popular poll says it is! Furthermore, God is not who experts, including college professors, say He is. This excludes the Christian church because the church reflects the same ancient, most validated manuscripts.

In other words, Truth is not *"what is comprehensible."* This idea is just another false view. It attempts to make the case that the view with the most data is true while those that are not as comprehensive are not true or not *as true*.

For example, when programs such as National Geographic or the Discovery Channel consistently feature top experts in its programming, it's an effort to depict its programming as being the most comprehensible, hence truthful. As a result, it is likely that most viewers will assume that most if not everything presented on these networks is *true* under the false assumption that these programs are the most comprehensible source. It is amazing to see these supposed experts speak to theories such as evolution as if it were fact and not theory—and people believe it because of the perception that such networks are the most comprehensive source!

While comprehensiveness is one test for truth, it does not determine the truth.[9] God is not defined by comprehensibility but the comprehensibility of God validates the true God as the only road to Heaven. Finally, not only is truth not what is comprehensible and God not based on who and what the secular experts say He is—truth is also not what feels good. God is not based on what makes us feel good.

Is The True God Found In What Makes Us Feel Good?

One of the most popular views today is that truth *is what feels good*. This belief holds that truth is found in our *subjective feelings*. The subjective view says that truth is what gives a satisfying feeling, whereas error is what gives a bad feeling—if it feels good it must be true and if it feels bad it must be false. This was popularized in the United States in the 1960s with the popular mantra, "If it feels good, do it!" Many in our society now believe this mantra and make it the centerpiece of how they choose which god they will follow. If Christianity is too restrictive for their taste, they might switch to or add in a bit of the *pantheistic* worldview, adapting beliefs of Hinduism or Buddhism into or in place of their Christian faith. After all, it feels better, so it must lead to the same spiritual Truth. The worldview for this type of thinking is called *hedonism*, or the pursuit of pleasure based on pursuing what feels good as the chief aim in life.

Living for what feels good as truth has three major problems. First, we as human beings are not very good judges for selecting what feels good. The human race often seeks pleasure in things like drugs, extramarital or premarital sex, and selfish ambition in the workplace or church (Philippians 1:15-18). As a result, we often miss the big picture regarding the truth, which is that true joy and pleasure are found only in authentic relationship with the almighty God of the universe through the person of Jesus Christ. Second, the mantra "if it feels good, do it" as truth cannot be trusted. Sinful, hedonistic living tastes good going down, but digests in our souls like rocks in our stomach. Being a Christian doesn't always feel good. Third, the view that "what feels good" as truth defies the thought of eternal life and Jesus Christ as the convincing indicator regarding life after death. God is truth, and to live according to the mantra, "if it feels good, do it" is to embrace our own selfish desires about who we want God to be, missing out on the real source of life's great joy and pleasure.

Sometimes bad news is good news because it allows us to correct error and redirect our actions in a wise and truthful way. Furthermore, feelings can be relative to individual personalities. What feels good to one person may not feel good to another. If truth were defined by feelings, then truth would not be objective. It would be changeable according to each person's personal taste and not unmovable according to an unchangeable God. It is clear that truth is *not* what feels good.[10]

Now that we have looked at what truth is not, let's turn our attention to *what truth is.*

Truth Is Transcultural—True for All Cultures

Truth is *transcultural.* Two plus two equals four for all people in all places, at all times for all cultures. Christian apologist Ravi Zacharias tells a story about a man who was upset with him because Ravi, being from India where 80 percent of the populous believes in Hinduism, now believes in Western theology. Ravi patiently conversed with the gentleman. He could see the man didn't understand, so finally, Ravi made his point through a simple illustration. If he, Ravi, were to step off the curb to cross the street during rush hour without looking for traffic, he would likely be hit by a bus or another vehicle, whether he were in New York City or New Delhi. In other words, just because you *think relatively* that it's true for you but not me that a bus will not hit you in India or in New York City, it's still absolutely true that you are going to suffer the consequences of a large bus or other vehicle despite your relative philosophical position. God is the same way. God is truth and truth is what corresponds to reality. To think relatively is to deny the truth, and that comes with eternal consequences, as you are going down a road that does not lead to Heaven. This is the truth for all people, in all places, and at all times. All truths are absolute truths, even though they may *appear* relative.[11]

Is Truth Invented or Discovered?

If truth never changes, will there ever be a time when there is never any new truth? The answer to that question is that while we *discover* new truths all the time, we don't *invent* new truth. Because God is omniscient (*knows all things*) and infinite (*without beginning or end*), it follows that He must know all truths from eternity. This includes everything there is, ever has been, or ever will be to know about our life (Luke 12:7; Matt. 10:30; 1 John 3:20), including the blueprints for the F-18 fighter plane or the Space Shuttle to every detail. If someone tells you that truth is invented, ask them if gravity existed prior to Sir Isaac Newton. Newton discovered the truth of gravity but he did not invent gravity itself. Truth exists independent of one's knowledge of it.[12] I cannot stress enough the importance of our understanding that truth is knowable, absolute, and attainable for each and every one of us. Because truth is knowable, God is knowable.

The Importance of Our Knowing the Truth

The importance of the nature of truth is critical to all people, especially to the Christian because Christianity is based on *absolute truth*—the absolute truth of God. God is *Truth*, and whatever is absolutely true is true for everyone, everywhere, at all times. Furthermore, Christianity claims that truth is *reality,* that which corresponds to *the way things really are.* The Christian claim that God exists means that there really is an *extracosmic Being* outside of the universe.[13] If we were unable to know truth then we would be unable to discern the truth about God or the differences between one religion and another. Logic and critical thought are essential to human understanding of truth and reality, and truth is the foundation of knowing all other things.

In generations past, it was unnecessary to explain the nature, meaning, and importance of truth. With the spread of relativism in this new age, it is essential for every person, especially within the church to be able to understand and address the meaning, nature, and importance of absolute truth. What truth *is* can be known, and because it can be known, the *truth* can be known. Furthermore, Jesus Christ proclaimed that He is the truth and the life, and that no one comes to the Father God except through Him. "Jesus answered, 'I am the way and the truth and the life. No one comes to the Father except through me" (John 14:6). In verse 7, Jesus goes on to proclaim that He is God. "If you really know me, you will know my Father as well. From now on, you do know him and have seen him" (John 14:7). Jesus said that by seeing Him we have seen God and that He, Jesus, is the Truth. This leads us to look at what the Bible says about Jesus being God and God being *the Truth*.

Questions For Reflection And Discussion

1. Why would anyone follow a God or a religion simply because it works for them?
2. Is truth what works?
3. Is it true that God is who everyone says He is?
4. Is God what one intends Him to be?
5. Is God who the experts say He is?
6. Is the true God found in what makes us feel good?
7. Is truth transcultural?
8. Is truth invented or discovered?
9. What is the importance of knowing the truth?

NOTES:

---

[1] Roy B. Zuck, *The Speakers Quote Book*, (Grand Rapids, Mich.: Kregel Publications, a division of Kregel, Inc., 7997), 402.

[2] Windfried Corduan, *A Christian Introduction to World Religions Neighboring Faiths*, (Downers Grove, Ill.: InterVarsity Press), copyright 1998, Windfried Corduan, 193.

[3] Kriteesh Parashar, thou shall be your own light, *Where does the count of 330 million Hindu Gods come from?* https://www.quora.com/Where-does-the-count-of-330-million-Hindu-Gods-come-from

[4] Windfried Corduan, 193.

[5] Geisler, *BECA*, 741.

[6] Raymond Hernandez, "Candidate's Words on Vietnam Service Differ From History," (*New York Times*, May 17, 2010, http://www.nytimes.com/2010/05/18/nyregion/18blumenthal.html?_r=1)

[7] Geisler, *BECA*, 741.

[8] Geisler, *BECA*, 741.

[9] Geisler, *BECA*, 741.

[10] Geisler, *BECA*, 742

[11] Norman L. Geisler and Frank Turek, *I Don't Have Enough Faith to Be An Atheist*, (Wheaton, Ill.: Crossway Books), copyright 2004, Norman L. Geisler and Frank Turek, 54-55.

[12] Geisler and Turek, *I Don't Have Enough Faith*, 37.

[13] Norman L. Geisler, *Baker Encyclopedia of Christian Apologetics*, (Grand Rapids, Mich.: Baker Books, 2000), 741.

CHAPTER 7

IS GOD THE ULTIMATE TRUTH?

"I am the way and the truth and the life. No one comes to the Father except through me." —Jesus Christ (John 14:6-7)

The first president of the United States and a devout Christian, President George Washington stated at the age of 15, "When you speak of God, and His attributes, let it be seriously and with reverence ..."[1]

George Washington understood that when we speak about God we are speaking about His character, or things that can be said of Him. One of God's attributes is truth. God is truth by His very nature. We as human beings *have* truth, but God *is* truth.[2] Truth is much more than simply information about God, but God Himself is truth.[3]

Furthermore, God is not only absolutely truthful, but He is *all good,* or *omnibenevolent.* Because God is omnibenevolent it is impossible for Him to lie. The Book of Hebrews tells us, "… so that by two unchangeable things, in which it is impossible for God to lie, we who have fled for refuge might have strong encouragement to hold fast to the hope set before us" (Hebrews 6:18, ESV). Because God cannot lie, it follows that everything God says is the truth.

Moreover, since God is truth and pure goodness, He is the ultimate standard for what is true, what is morally right. And God's function as the ultimate standard demands His perfection. In setting this standard, He is also the ultimate Lawgiver. The ultimate measure of truth is by its very nature perfect; hence, God is perfect. For God can be no less perfect than a yardstick can be less than three feet long.[4] Because God is perfect and cannot lie, we can be absolutely sure that He *is* the truth and His Word *speaks* the truth.

To deny truth is to deny God. Relativism in general denies the existence of God, including His exclusivity and moral guidelines, which are provided in Scripture as valid, knowable, and absolutely true. To embrace relativism is to deny the existence of God, which leads to the denial of God as the truth. A relative view of God leads to a relative view of truth.

The denial of truth as absolute affects one's daily life in many ways, including work relationships, political views, and most especially marriage. How can a wife trust her husband or a husband trust his wife when absolute truth is denied or ignored? How can an employer trust an employee's witness of Jesus Christ if that employee demonstrates wrongful behavior in order to enrich his or her personal desires?

If we deny truth, the effects are very real. It brings into question our faith in one God versus the concept of all roads leading to Heaven. How can we live out our Christian faith according to the Word of God if truth is relative? If we accept truth as relative, we will embrace religious pluralism and accept all things said of morality as relative. We will accept all Scripture, from Genesis to Revelation, as relative, including the Ten Commandments. If the Ten Commandments are relative, then all of God's moral commands are relative. If we accept God's commands as relative, what would be our response to the concept of God as the only way to Heaven? We would have no real response to give. In such a case, we would have no real reason to complain about the violations committed in the name of religion. We could not complain about the behavior of our politicians, or the lack of morality in our culture or in our children's lives.

As Christians, we ought to be proactively persuading our friends, co-workers, and family of the exclusive truth of God's Word and His design for our life. By doing so, we are fulfilling Jesus' call for us to be salt and light in our world (Matthew 5:13-16).

Evidence Confirming God's Perfection (Absolute Truthfulness)

Truth is telling it like it is, whereas in steep contrast, falsehood is telling it like it isn't. We are commanded to be truthful: "... but your yes

is to be yes, and your no, no, so that you may not fall under judgment"
(James 5:12, NASB). Lying opposes the truth: "I have not written to
you because you do not know the truth, but because you do know it,
and because no lie is of the truth" (1 John 2:21, NASB). The devil is
the father of all lies (John 8:44). God on the other hand cannot lie (2
Corinthians 1:18; Titus 1:2; Hebrews 6:18).

Scripture Verses Illustrating God's Absolute Truthfulness:[5]

- **Numbers 23:19:** *"God is not a man, that He should lie,
  nor a son of man, that He should change His mind. Does
  He speak and then not act? Does He promise and not
  fulfill?"* (NIV).

- **Psalm 31:5:***"Into Your hands I commit my spirit; redeem
  me, O Lord, the God of truth."* (NIV).

- **Psalm 33:4:** *"For the word of the Lord is right and true;
  He is faithful in all He does"* (NIV).

- **John 14:6:** *"Jesus answered, 'I am the Way and the Truth
  and the Life. No one comes to the Father except through
  me'"* (NIV).

- **John 4:24**: *"God is spirit, and those who worship him
  must worship in sprit and truth"* (ESV).

- **Other references:** Deuteronomy 32:4; 1 Thessalonians
  1:9; John 15:26; and 1 John 4:1-6.

Theological Evidence for God's Truthfulness

God's truthfulness follows from His other attributes, such as His *immutability,* the fact that He is unchangeable in nature; and His *infinity, which means He is* without limits. Because God is truthful, He must be truthful in accordance with His nature. Because He is immutable, God must be unchangeably truthful. The Bible illustrates this point in 2 Timothy 2:13: "If we are faithless, he remains faithful—for he cannot deny himself" (ESV). Because God is infinite and because He is truthful, it follows that He must be infinitely truthful. And whoever is infinitely truthful cannot be partly truthful but must be wholly and completely truthful.[6]

The fact that God is absolutely truthful requires that He cannot lie because absolute truth is absolute, leaving no exceptions for non-truth. God is limited by His nature in that it is impossible for Him to lie because that would conflict with His truth nature, thus excluding Him from being an all-perfect and truthful God. God cannot lie because He is truth and thus limited to only telling the truth.

Evidence from Logic: God Is Truth and Truthful

God's absolute truthfulness flows from several of His other attributes. If God is truthful, then He must be truthful in accordance to His nature. Because God is a simple being (pure spirit and without parts), and indivisible by nature, He cannot be partly anything. Whatever He is, it is necessary that He must be totally and completely just that. It is impossible for God to be in part or even possess truth because He *is* truth and His word is completely and totally truthful.

Understanding what truth is becomes very important in our pursuit of the true God of the universe. An excellent example of defining truth, "telling it like it is" was well illustrated when Pilate asked Jesus, "What is truth?" in John 18:38. The fact that Pilate asked that question indicates that he knew some truth. Furthermore, by exonerating Jesus, Pilate was *telling it like it is.*[7]

A.W. Tozer spoke more deeply to the importance of God as truth and goodness and how that works in our daily lives. In his book *Knowledge of the Holy,* Tozer said, "The greatness of God rouses fear within us, but His goodness encourages us not to be afraid of Him. To fear and not be afraid—that is the paradox of faith."[8] This is a beautiful picture of God's goodness, justice, power, and mercy in His wanting us to abide by the good moral boundaries that flow from His very nature. To say that truth is relative is to say that God is relative.

Acknowledging the possibility of absolute truth brings sudden death to one's relativistic worldview, forbidding him or her the freedom to deny the very real existence of God and to live life thinking that all roads lead to Heaven. It prohibits a person from sporting the COEXIST bumper sticker while unknowingly driving down the road to eternal ruin. There are many ways to Jesus but only One way to Heaven. The evidence in the Scriptures, namely the New Testament, is proven superior to every other book of antiquity. If these Scriptures are superior and the truth, then Jesus is true. Therefore, Christianity is the exclusive Truth.

Questions For Reflection And Discussion
1. Who is the only person to claim that he is God and the Truth?
2. What are some biblical evidences confirming God's perfection?
3. List three biblical Scriptures illustrating God's absolute truthfulness?
4. What theological evidences are there for God's truthfulness?
5. What logical evidence is there for God's truthfulness?

NOTES:

[1] William J. Federer, *America's God and Country Encyclopedia of Quotations* by. Quotation taken from 1745: 110 Rules of Civility and Decent Behavior in Company and Conversation (copied in his own handwriting at the age of 15), Bedford, MA: Apple Books, 1988, distributed by The Glove Pequot Press, Chester, Conn.), p. 30 Moncure D. Conway, George Washington's Rules of Civility (1890), pp. 178, 180. William J. Johnson, George Washington-The Christian (St. Paul, Minn: William J. Johnson Merriam Park, February ... See p. 821 of Federer's book for rest of source.

[2] Norman L. Geisler, *Systematic Theology in One Volume*, (Bloomington, Minn.: Bethany House Publishers, 2011), 581.

[3] Bromiley, *International Standard Bible*, 928.

[4] Geisler, *Notes*, Chapter 14, p. 4.

[5] Geisler *Notes*, Chapter 15, 1.

[6] Norman L. Geisler, *Systematic Theology in One Volume*, (Bloomington, Minn.: Bethany House Publishers, 201), 582.

[7] Norman L. Geisler and Frank Turek, 36-37.

[8] A.W. Tozer, *The Knowledge of the Holy*, (New York, N.Y.: HarperSanFrancisco, 1961), 84.

CHAPTER 8

IS THERE HISTORICAL EVIDENCE ABOUT JESUS OUTSIDE OF THE BIBLE?

"Now there was about this time Jesus, a wise man, if it be lawful to call him a man; for he was a doer of wonderful works, a teacher of such men as receive the truth with pleasure. He drew over to him both many of the Jews and many of the Gentiles. He was [the] Christ. And when Pilate, at the suggestion of the principal men amongst us, had condemned him to the cross, those that loved him at the first did not forsake him; for he appeared to them alive again the third day; as the divine prophets had foretold these and ten thousand other wonderful things concerning him. And the tribe of Christians, so named from him, are not extinct at this day."[1]
— ***Flavius Josephus*** — *1ˢᵗ Century Historian on the Scene 37A.D., Antiquities, Book 18, chapter 3, paragraph 3.*

When I first moved to the Carolinas in the late 1990's, I made a new friend at the YMCA by the name of Kent. Kent grew up in a Christian church with a Christian worldview, but he had more of a cultural understanding of Christianity. When Kent went off to fight in the Vietnam War, his worldview began to change. He began to question the existence of an all-good God, particularly in light of the atrocities of war.

Kent became skeptical about the validity of the Bible as the true Word of God and Jesus Christ as God's Son. Having spent time in the Asian culture, he was exposed to the predominant religions of Vietnam, most notably Vietnamese folk religion, Confucianism, Buddhism, and Taoism. Vietnam is one of the least religious countries in the world.

According to an official 2014 government survey of 24 million Vietnamese, 11 million are traditional Buddhists; 6.2 million are Catholic; 4.4 million are Caodaists, which is a Vietnamese form of Monism; 1.4 million are Protestants; and 1.3 million are Hoahaoists, an independent form of Buddhism founded in 1939. There are 75,000 Muslims, 7,000 Bahais, 1,500 Hindus and other smaller groups.[2] Furthermore, the Socialist Republic of Vietnam is an Atheist state as declared by its communist government.[3]

Coming Into The Light

Kent was unprepared for the plethora of worldviews and diversity of religions that he was thrust into. Trying to make sense of it, he adopted a view that all religions lead to the same spiritual truth. In other words, all roads can lead to Heaven.

Prior to the Vietnam War, the general U.S. population attended church and believed in the Bible as the inerrant word of God. Upon Kent's return from Vietnam, the country had changed. The war protests, sexual revolution, and recreational drugs led to the rejection of authority, including God, parents, and government. As culture began turning against the Bible and the person of Jesus Christ as the Son of God, so did Kent. He didn't understand why Jesus was superior to other gods or why the Bible was superior to other ancient religious documents.

Ten years after I met Kent at that rural strip mall YMCA, I saw him for the last time. At the beginning of our friendship, he had admitted that he was *agnostic* (not certain about the existence of God) at best. But this last time I saw him, something interesting happened. After a decade of countless conversations about world religions and worldviews, Kent's mind was beginning to see the truth about God. On this particular day, he was working out on a weight machine about 15 feet away from me when I noticed him motioning for me to come over.

He looked me in the eyes and said, "Steve, how do you know?"

"What do you mean?" I asked.

I didn't want to make any assumptions.

"Steve, you know what I mean!" Now I was sure of his question. He wanted to know how a person could know with absolute certainty that God exists. The Holy Spirit gave me a great illustration.

"Kent, you served in the Vietnam War, correct?

"Yes sir, I did."

"Can you remember being in the middle of a rice paddy field in the pitch black night?

"Yes, Steven, all too well."

"Imagine one of those nights when you could see nothing but pitch black." I paused a few seconds. "What did you do?"

"I kept my eyes open for some way out."

"You kept scanning the horizon until you could identify some speck of light. And what did you do when you found that light?"

"I moved in that direction."

"What happened as you got closer to the speck of light?"

"It got bigger," he said.

That's the answer I was looking for. "As a matter of fact, eventually the light was large and bright enough to illuminate your way to a place of safety, right?"

Kent's eyes widened. "Yes. And I finally made my way back to base."

"And when you arrived, you were 'in the light' and under the protection of your base unit. Kent, that is how you know."

His face looked as if scales had fallen from his eyes. He asked no more questions. He simply extended his arm, shook my hand firmly and said: "Steve, I get it … I finally get it! Thank you very much." That conversation brought full circle ten years of dialog regarding biblical, philosophical, and theological evidence confirming the New Testament as the most validated ancient document in the world and Jesus Christ as the only way to God the Father.

The Importance of Extra-Biblical Evidence Supporting the Validity of the Scriptures

My ten-year conversation with Kent highlights the importance of using extra-biblical evidence to validate biblical Scriptures as the ultimate Truth. Kent wanted to know why the biblical Scriptures are *the truth* and other religious documents about different gods are not true. He wanted to know the difference between worldviews and the different world religions. He wanted to know philosophically and evidentially why Christianity is the truth. In order for us to be effective in responding to *religious pluralism*, we must be able to show extra-biblical evidence, philosophical evidence, and theological evidence, as well as simple logic.

Most people don't know that historical evidence for the life of Christ exists outside the Bible. One of these sources is the famous Jewish historian *Flavius Josephus* (ca. A.D. 37-ca. 100). Josephus was a Jewish historian and a Pharisee who confirmed in both general terms and with great detail the historical accounts of the Old Testament and some of the New Testament. Josephus also supported what would become the Protestant view of the Canon of the Old Testament. In his writings, Josephus referred to Jesus as the brother of James who was martyred, and he confirmed the martyrdom of John the Baptist.[4]

The historical accounts written by Josephus in his book *Antiquities* include the following:

1) **John the Baptist and King Herod—Book 18, chapter 5 paragraph 2.** (116) "Now some of the Jews thought that the destruction of Herod's army came from God, and that very justly, as a punishment of what he did against John, that was called the Baptist: (117) for Herod slew him, who was a good man, and commanded the Jews to exercise virtue, both as to righteousness towards one another, and piety towards God, and so to come to baptism; for that the washing [with water] would be acceptable to him, if they made use of it, not in order to the putting away [or the remission] of some sins [only], but for the purification of the body; supposing still that the soul was thoroughly purified beforehand by righteousness."[5]

2) **Jesus—Book 18, chapter 3, paragraph 3.** (63) "Now there was about this time Jesus, a wise man, if it be lawful to call him a man; for he was a doer of wonderful works, a teacher of such men as receive the truth with pleasure. He drew over to him both many of the Jews and many of the Gentiles. He was [the] Christ. (64) And when Pilate,

at the suggestion of the principal men amongst us, had condemned him to the cross, those that loved him at the first did not forsake him; for he appeared to them alive again the third day; as the divine prophets had foretold these and ten thousand other wonderful things concerning him. And the tribe of Christians, so named from him, is not extinct at this day.[6]

3) **James, the brother of Jesus—Book 20, chapter 9, paragraph 1.** "Festus was now dead, and Albinus was but upon the road; so he assembled the Sanhedrin of judges, and brought before them the brother of Jesus, who was called Christ, whose name was James, and some others [or, some of his companions]; and when he had formed an accusation against them as breakers of the law, he delivered them to be stoned: (201) but as for those who seemed the most equitable of the citizens, and such as were the most uneasy at the breach of the laws, they disliked what was done."[7]

4) **Ananias the High Priest, who ordered those standing near Paul to strike him on the mouth in Acts 23:2—Book 20, chapter 9, paragraph 2** (204) "Now as soon as Albinus was come to the city of Jerusalem, he used all his endeavors and care that the country might be kept in peace, and this by destroying many of the *Sicarii* (205). But as for the high priest, Ananias, he increased in glory every day, and this to a great degree, and had obtained the favor and esteem of the citizens in a signal manner; for he was a great hoarder up of money ..."[8]

Other Extra-Biblical Writings as Evidence Supporting the Bible

If critics discount Josephus as a source because of his Jewish origin, there are other secular writers who have verified details of Jesus' life. One of the first non-Jewish secular writers who wrote of Jesus was Thallus, a Samaritan-born historian who lived and worked in Rome about 52 A.D. Thallus wrote a history of the Eastern Mediterranean world, from the Trojan War up to his own time. Though his writings now exist only in fragments cited by other writers, they still provide strong validation for the life of Jesus Christ. One writer who cited Thallus was *Julius Africanus*, a Christian whose work dates back to around A.D. 221.

In one passage, Africanus refers to a comment made by Thallus regarding the darkness that enveloped the land during the later afternoon hours the day Jesus died on the cross. Thallus explains away the darkness as an eclipse of the sun. Africanus noted that Thallus' assertion was unreasonable because a solar eclipse could not take place at the time of the full moon, and the time of the crucifixion came at the season of the Paschal full moon.[9]

This affirmation of the darkness surrounding Jesus' crucifixion is just one of many details from Jesus' life that can be found in extra-biblical sources. As the internal and external evidence begins to mount, we can see *light* shining through the puncture holes of arguments by nonbelievers who say the Bible is just a made-up story. For further evidence on Jesus' life, I recommend reading Josh McDowell's book *The New Evidence that Demands a Verdict*.

Now that we have shown extra-biblical evidence for the Bible, let's turn our attention to some important biblical evidence that will show beyond a reasonable doubt that All Roads Don't Lead To Heaven.

Questions For Reflection And Discussion

1. Why are the extra-biblical evidences supporting the validation of the Scriptures important?
2. Who is Josephus and what was one of his famous books supporting facts about Jesus written in the Scriptures?
3. What are three examples of the work of Josephus that support the Bible?
4. Who is Thallus and Julius Africanus?
5. When did Thallus live and what did he write about?
6. What is one of the very important things about the Resurrection of Jesus that Thallus wrote about?

NOTES:

[1] Flavius, *The New Complete Works of*, 590.

[2] https://www.gov.uk/government/uploads/system/uploads/attachment_data/file/389940/CIG.Vietnam.Religious_Minority_Groups.v1.0.pdf

[3] Jan Dodd, Mark Lewis, Ron Emmons. *The Rough Guide to Vietnam, Vol. 4, 2003. p. 509: "After 1975, the Marxist-Leninist government of reunified Vietnam declared the state atheist while theoretically allowing people the right to practice their religion under the constitution."*

[4] Josh McDowell, *The New Evidence*, 122.

[5] Flavius Josephus, *The New Complete Works of Josephus Translated by William Whiston*, Commentary by Paul L. Maier, (Grand Rapids, Mich.: Kregel Publishers, 1999.), 595.

[6] Flavius, *The New Complete Works of*, 590.

[7] Flavius, *The New Complete Works of*, 656.

[8] Flavius, *The New Complete Works of*, 656-657.

[9] McDowell, *The New Evidence*, 122.

CHAPTER 9

IS JESUS THE ONLY ROAD TO HEAVEN?

"Thomas said to him, 'Lord, we don't know where you are going, so how can we know the way?' Jesus answered, 'I am the way and the truth and the life. No one comes to the Father except through me.'" —Jesus Christ (John 14:5-6)

Jesus—Lord, Liar, or Lunatic?

In his bestselling book *More Than A Carpenter* Christian apologist Josh McDowell writes that many people regard Jesus not as God but as a good man, a moral man—an exceptionally wise prophet who spoke many truths. But Josh makes this emphatic point: Jesus has to fit one of three categories. Either He is a liar, a lunatic, or He is who He said He was, the Lord.[1]

Someone who lived as Jesus lived His life, and taught what Jesus taught, and died as Jesus died could not have been a liar. That being the case, Josh pushes his reader to consider the next alternative—Is it possible that Jesus Christ was deranged or crazy in thinking that He was God? Was He a lunatic? It is difficult to categorize Jesus as mentally disturbed when you consider the content of His message and the authority He carried. He spoke the most profound words ever recorded, and His instructions have liberated countless people who were in mental bondage. This leaves us with the last option: perhaps Jesus was who He said He was—the Lord God Himself. The apostle John wrote, "These are written that you may believe that Jesus is the Messiah, the Son of God, and that by believing you may have life in his name" (John 20:31). The evidence is clearly against classifying Jesus as liar or lunatic. It greatly supports Jesus as Lord and Savior.[2]

Let's now look at three additional lines of evidence supporting Jesus as Lord and Savior. First, we will look at biblical prophecy about the coming of the Messiah. Second, we will look at evidence confirming the truthfulness of the New Testament writers. Third, we will look at the New Testament as the most validated and recorded ancient document in all of history.

PROPHECY AS PROOF OF THE BIBLE

Prophecy is one of, if not *the greatest,* testimony that Jesus was in fact who He said He was: Lord and Savior, the one and only road to Heaven. One of the strongest evidences that the Bible is inspired by God is its predictive prophecy. Unlike any other book or religious document, the Bible offers a plethora of very specific predictions. Many of these prophecies were made hundreds of years in advance and were literally fulfilled or pointed to a definite future time when those prophetic predictions would come true.[3]

The Encyclopedia of Biblical Prophecies calculated that 27 percent of the Bible contains predictive prophecies (Payne, 675). No other book in the world can make this claim. This is a sure sign of the divine origin of the Bible,[4] and it proves the Bible's superiority over all other ancient manuscripts, including any and all religious texts. Because all of these prophecies pertain to the coming Messiah, and Jesus fulfilled all of them literally and perfectly, this further validates the New Testament as the truth and Jesus Christ as the Messiah.

Let's now turn our attention to some biblical characters and how their stories provide an even greater abundance of evidence for the credibility of the New Testament and the New Testament writers.

PROPHECIES

God provided prophets to speak about things mankind should watch for in order to recognize and believe the Messiah when he did arrive. These prophecies, or predicted signs, were given to us in the Old Testament, which is the part of the Bible written prior to the birth of Jesus. The Old Testament (Jewish Torah) was completed in 450 B.C., hundreds of years before the birth of Jesus, and it contains more than 300 prophecies that Jesus fulfilled through His life, death, and resurrection.

The mathematical odds of any one person fulfilling this number of prophecies are staggering.

- One person fulfilling eight prophecies: one in 100,000,000,000,000,000.
- One person fulfilling 48 prophecies: one chance in 10 to the 157th power.
- One person fulfilling 300+ prophecies: so many zeroes that it would engulf the page with ink. Simply put, only Jesus!

  This is a magnificent testimony to the fact that the Bible is the one and only truly, inspired Word of God, the one and only book that leads to the one and only Spiritual Truth.[5]

In the New Testament the apostles attested to the life of Jesus and His messiahship. One part focuses on the Resurrection and the other on fulfilling messianic prophesy. The Old Testament was written over a one-thousand-year period and contains nearly three hundred references to the coming Messiah. All of these were fulfilled in Jesus Christ, and they establish strong validation of His credentials as the Messiah.[6]

Some Old Testament Prophecies Fulfilled In The New Testament

In Isaiah 9:1, prophecy tells us that the Messiah's ministry would begin in Galilee, and Matthew 4:12, 13 and 17 bear that out. Genesis 49:10 and Micah 5:2 predict that the Messiah would be from the Tribe of Judah, and Luke 3:23 and 33 bring that to pass. Micah 5:2 predicts the Messiah would be born in Bethlehem, and Matthew 2:1 proves that to be the case. Psalm 2:7 predicts that the Messiah is the Son of God. Matthew 3:17; 16:16, Mark 9:7; Luke 9:35; 22:70; Acts 13:30-33; and John 1:34, 49 fulfill that prophecy. "And suddenly a voice came from heaven saying, 'This is My beloved Son, in whom I am well pleased" (Mark 9:7).

Isaiah 7:14 predicts that the Messiah would be born of a virgin and Matthew 1:18, 24-25 fulfill that prophesy. "She was found with child of the Holy Spirit ... Then Joseph ... did not know her till she had brought forth her firstborn Son. And he called His name Jesus." Zechariah 11:12 predicts that the Messiah would be betrayed for thirty pieces of silver. We see the fulfillment of this prophecy in Matthew 26:15, when the apostle Judas asks: "What are you willing to give me if I deliver Him to you? And they counted out to him thirty pieces of silver" (Matt. 26:15). Psalm 22:18 predicts someone would cast lots for the Messiah's garments on the day he was crucified, and we see that in John 19:23-24.

Zechariah 12:10 predicted that the Messiah's side would be pierced, and that was fulfilled in John 19:34. Amos 8:9 predicted that darkness would take over the land, and that was fulfilled in Matthew 27:45: "Now from the sixth hour until the ninth hour there was darkness over all the land." Isaiah 53:9 predicted the Messiah would be buried in a rich man's tomb and Matthew 27:57-60 tells us, "There came a rich man from Arimathea, named Joseph ... and [he] asked for the body of Jesus." When Joseph had taken the body, he wrapped it in a clean linen cloth, and laid it in his new tomb" (Matt. 27:57-60).[7]

Biblical Evidence Confirming the Truthfulness of the Biblical Writers and Jesus Christ

In their book *I Don't Have Enough Faith to Be an Atheist,* authors Norman Geisler and Frank Turek give the *top ten reasons we know the*

New Testament writers told the truth. In evaluating biblical evidence, we gain a clearer picture of the validity of the New Testament based on a close examination of the New Testament itself. More specifically, we learn about the writers of the New Testament and whether or not they seem to be trustworthy sources.

The goal is to find out whether the Scriptural account of Jesus Christ is true. Affirming the truth of the New Testament is paramount to affirming that Jesus Christ is God. Let's look at a brief summary of five of Geisler and Turek's top ten reasons.

Five Reasons We Know the New Testament Writers Told the Truth

1) The New Testament writers, many of whom were disciples, included embarrassing details about themselves, such as the disciples running away while the women ran out to see the empty tomb first. The fact that these writers would include such details defies both logic and human nature. How often do you see politicians and religious leaders or even your co-workers put their mistakes, misspeak(s), and embarrassing moments into writing? The New Testament writers were committed to telling the truth. They reported clearly and honestly what they saw and what they did.[8]

2) The New Testament writers further show commitment to the truth by carefully distinguishing Jesus' words from their own, despite the fact that quotations were not part of

the literary rules of writing in first-century Greek. Most
red-letter editions of the Bible are identical in highlight-
ing the words of Jesus, thus illustrating just how easy the
New Testament writers made it to distinguish their own
words from those of Jesus.[9]

3) The New Testament authors included more than thirty
historically confirmed people in their writings. Had the
New Testament writers made up lies about these historical figures, it would have impeached their own credibility. They would have been judged and sentenced in the
court of public opinion by their own contemporary au-
diences for implicating real people in a fictional story,
especially since so many of the people they wrote about
were well-known and often in positions of great power. It
would have been impossible for the New Testament writers to get away with writing so many false stories about
figures such as *Pilate, Caiaphas, Festus, Felix,* and the
entire *Herodian* bloodline. Somebody would have exposed them and set the record straight. But this did not
happen for one simple reason: The New Testament writers were speaking the truth, and what they were saying
corresponded to reality.[10]

4) Many critics, past and present, have been all too eager
to point out what they perceive as contradictions in the
Gospel accounts. A common objective to the validity of
the New Testament is the perceived conflict in the Gospel
accounts of the empty tomb. Matthew says there was one

angel at the tomb of Jesus whereas John mentions two. If these accounts are contradictory, it is reasonable to question the validity of the New Testament. But this is a case of only *divergent details*, which serves to strengthen, not weaken, this eyewitness account.

Matthew does *not* say there was *only* one angel at the tomb. The critic would have to add the word *only* to the text in order to claim a contradiction between Matthew's account and John's testimony. The reason that Matthew would mention only one angel is the same reason that journalists covering the same event might choose to include different details in reporting their stories. Two independent eyewitnesses rarely see all the details the same and never describe the same event using the same exact words. The fact that both accounts mention there is at least one angel adds to the credibility of the overall story and of the eyewitness accounts of Matthew and John. The evidence only serves to strengthen the credibility, authenticity, and accuracy of the New Testament eyewitness accounts as they are recorded in the Bible.[11]

5) The New Testament writers go so far as to challenge their readers to check out the veracity of their words. For example, Luke testifies that his writings were derived from careful investigation. In his words to *Theophilus* in Luke 1:1-4, he specifically states that he was careful to order the details and content of his writings with both accuracy and verifiability. In 2 Peter 1:16, Peter makes the point that he and the other disciples did not follow cleverly devised stories but were literal eyewitnesses to the majesty of Jesus Christ.

And the Apostle Paul, who boldly proclaimed the resurrected Christ to Festus and King Agrippa in Acts chapter 26, reminds his readers in Second Corinthians that he previously performed miracles for them: "The signs of a true apostle were performed among you with utmost patience, with signs and wonders and mighty works" (2 Corinthians 12:12, ESV). It would have destroyed Paul's credibility with the Corinthians if he had claimed to do miracles that they had never seen him do. The best explanation is that Paul really did, in fact, do these miracles, thus confirming his apostleship.[12]

While these five reasons from Dr. Norman Geisler and Frank Turek do not exhaust the amount of biblical evidence available for affirming the New Testament and the life of Jesus Christ, they do serve as a good example of how apologetics can build up our faith and help us fulfill the Great Commission.

The New Testament is the Most Validated and Recorded Ancient Document in all of History

Geisler and Turek go on to address the number of New Testament manuscripts compared to other ancient documents, as well as the span of time between the original writings and the first surviving copies. For example, the gap between the original and first surviving copies of other ancient writers is as follows: The gap for Pliny was 400 years; Caesar, 950 years; Tacitus, 750-950 years; Plato, 1,300; Herodotus 1,350; Demosthenes 1,100; and Homer, 400. However, the gap for the New Testament was only 25 years.[13] The significance of this relatively small time gap is that eyewitnesses to Jesus Christ would have been still alive 25 years later and could have challenged the writings of the New Testament if they weren't true.

How Many Copies of Each Ancient Manuscript Actually Exists?

Regarding the number of manuscript copies for these ancient documents, Geisler and Turek found the following: There are 200 manuscript copies for Pliny the Elder, 251 for Caesar, 2+31 15C copies for Tacitus, 210 for Plato, 109 for Herodotus, 340 for Demosthenes, 1,800 for Homer, and at last count, 5,838 Greek New Testament Manuscripts dating (50-100 AD). There is a total of 18,524 Greek New Testament Early Translations plus 42,000 manuscript copies for the Old Testament. When you add 5,838 New Testament Greek manuscripts with 18,524 copies of the New Testament early translations plus 42,000 Old Testament Scrolls and Codices, it totals 66,362. We are still finding additional copies of at least portions of the New Testament manuscripts each year.[14] Having such a large number of copies to compare aids in our confidence that our translations of the Bible are accurately conveying the right message. If you would like to learn more about these claims, I would encourage you to read Geisler and Turek's book, *I Don't Have Enough Faith to Be an Atheist.*

The Importance of Having the Most Ancient and Validated Manuscripts

The point of being aware of the evidence from these manuscripts is to help us verify the truth of who Christ is. If we understand that God is truth, and Jesus Christ claimed to be God, then, we know Jesus Christ claimed to be Truth. And in this fog of relativism in which we live, we have to validate the ancient manuscripts in order to validate the claims of Jesus Christ, particularly that He is the Truth (John 14:6). So being able to verify the New Testament empowers us to defend what the New Testament says about Christ. And we often find that we cannot speak about salvation through Jesus Christ until we validate the New Testament Scriptures because of the lack of biblical knowledge and general acceptance of relativism among so many people today.

Now in some cases, before we can even talk about Scripture, we must first validate the existence of God. And in still other cases, before we can even establish the existence of God, we must establish if *truth can be known* in the first place. You see, if we can't establish that truth can be known, we cannot know that God, knowledge in general, or the ability to know anything actually exists. If we cannot show that truth is absolute and validate the existence of God, and then the Bible—which is all about God's interaction with mankind throughout *His*-story—then any talk about Jesus Christ meets with a lack of understanding in the mind of the hearer.

As a result, our efforts become more diluted. If the validity of the Bible becomes an obstacle that Christians cannot overcome with a good answer, our efforts in evangelism and personal growth in Jesus Christ will be severely limited. If we are unable to give a reason for the validity of the biblical Scriptures, then our talk about Jesus Christ will become less valid in the eyes of the person with whom we are attempting to share our faith. It is at this point that many concede to the belief that *all religions lead to Heaven* and slap that COEXIST bumper sticker on the back of their vehicle.

There Are Many Ways To Jesus, But Jesus Is The Only Way To Heaven

Jesus claimed to be the truth. In John 14:6, Jesus said: "I am the way and the truth and the life. No one comes to the Father except through me." Jesus went on to say in chapter 10: "I tell you the truth, the man who does not enter the sheep pen by the gate, but climbs in by some other way, is a thief and a robber … I am the gate; whoever enters through me will be saved" (John 10: 1-9).

Jesus' disciples spoke to Jesus as truth. Acts 4:12 says, "Salvation is found in no one else, for there is no other name under Heaven given to men by which we must be saved." And 1Timothy 2:5 says, "For there is one God and one mediator between God and men, the man Christ Jesus …"

Jesus proved that He is the truth by fulfilling more than one hundred ancient prophecies, by living a sinless and miraculous life, by His death on the cross and His resurrection from the dead. No other religious leader or figure did this! There are many ways to Christ, but Christ is the only way to God. The Bible is 100 percent right and the progressive physics of secular humanism is wrong—because Jesus claimed to be the only way, and He proved in three miraculous ways that He truly is the only way to God. While religious pluralism challenges the biblical claim that Jesus Christ is the only way to God the Father and to Heaven, its challenges fail to hold weight.

First, Jesus satisfied God's unchanging call for justice. Jesus was the only sacrificial lamb and gave His life freely to satisfy payment for our inequities. Because of the death of Christ, we are made right, or justified, before God as if we have never sinned.

Second, it is impossible for sinful man to satisfy God's justice. Christ's absolute righteousness alone is able to satisfy, or propitiate, the just demands of an absolutely righteous God. Furthermore, Christ's righteousness is imputed to those who believe in Him as the only way to fulfill the righteous demands of the law (Romans 8:3-4).[15]

Third, we simply cannot do it on our own. No human being outside of Jesus Christ has ever lived a perfect life, making it impossible for any of us to satisfy God's perfect justice. How about those who sincerely try? Sincerity is not a test for truth, and any of us can be sincerely wrong (Proverbs 14:12). Remember the Titanic? The craftsmen of the ship sincerely thought it was unsinkable, and as it turned out it wasn't.

Those who seek the true light will find it. "Truly I understand that God shows no partiality, but in every nation anyone who fears him and does what is right is accepted to him" (Acts 10:34-35, ESV). "And without faith it is impossible to please God, because anyone who comes to him must believe that he exists and that he rewards those who earnestly seek him" (Hebrews 11:6).[16]

Questions For Reflection And Discussion

1. What percent of the Bible contains predictive prophesies according to the Encyclopedia of Biblical Prophesies?
2. Why is this important and what does it prove?
3. What are the mathematical odds of any one person fulfilling more than 300 prophecies as Jesus Christ did?
4. Give at least three very specific and clear prophesies that Jesus fulfilled?
5. What are five reasons that we know the New Testament writers told the truth?
6. What evidence do we have that the New Testament is the most validated recorded ancient document in all of history?

NOTES:

¹ Josh McDowell, *More Than A Carpenter*, (Wheaton, Illinois Tyndale House Publishers, 2004), 22.

² IBID. 24-31.

³ Geisler, BECA, 609.

⁴ Geisler, BECA, 617.

⁵ CBN, *Biblical Prophecies Fulfilled by Jesus*, www.CBN.Com (http://www1.cbn.com/biblestudy/biblical-prophecies-fulfilled-by-jesus)

⁶ IBID. 164.

⁷ IBID. 168-193.

⁸ Norman L. Geisler and Frank Turek, *I Don't Have Enough Faith to Be an Atheist*, (Wheaton, Ill.: Crossway Books), Copyright Norman L. Geisler and Frank Turek, 277.

⁹ Geisler and Turek, *I Don't Have Enough Faith*, 281.

¹⁰ Geisler, *I Don't Have*, 283-284.

¹¹ Geisler, *I Don't Have*, 284.

¹² Geisler, *I Don't Have*, 286-287.

¹³ I Geisler, *I Don't Have*, 226.

¹⁴ Geisler, *I Don't Have*, 226.

¹⁵ Norman Geisler, *Systematic Theology Volume Two God Creation*, (Minneapolis, Minn.: Bethany House Publishers, 2003), 333.

¹⁶ Norman Geisler, *Pluralism*, Powerpoint classroom presentation, 2005, Slide 6.

Chapter 10

HOW DO I KNOW THAT I AM GOING TO HEAVEN?

"Your salvation depends on what [Christ] has done for you, not on what you do for Him. It isn't your hold on God that saves you; it's His hold on you." — Billy Graham[1]

Can I Really Know That I Am Going To Heaven?

Yes, absolutely. We can be sure about where we will spend eternity when we pass from this earth and leave our earthen body. We can know with certainty that when we die, we will go to heaven. How can we be sure? This is a question that many people have struggled with, especially folks who are seeking God or who are new believers in Jesus Christ.

The Bible outlines how to have peace with God—it comes only through Jesus Christ. Most people have an idea of what they believe it will take to be accepted by God. After all, who likes the idea of exiting this life without being on good terms with him? Thankfully, it's possible to be certain that you've made peace with God, but the way must be chosen during this life. Here are the steps drawn from God's book the Bible laid out by the Billy Graham Evangelistic Association.

Steps to Peace with God:

The Bible teaches that the assurance of salvation rests securely upon four unshakable pillars:

Step 1. Understand God's purposes—peace and eternal life

God loves you and wants you to experience peace and an eternal, fulfilling life.

The Bible says...

"We have peace with God through our Lord Jesus Christ." *Romans 5:1*

"For God so loved the world, that he gave his only Son, that whoever believes in him should not perish but have eternal life." *John 3:16*

"I came that they may have life and have it abundantly." *John 10:10*

Why don't most people have this peace and the fulfilling (abundant) life that God intended for us to have?

Step 2. Admit the problem—our sin and separation

God did not create us like robots to automatically love and mechanically obey him. God gave us a will and the freedom to choose. The first man and woman chose to disobey God and go their own willful way. And we still make that choice today. This results in separation from God.

The Bible says...

"For all have sinned and fall short of the glory of God." *Romans 3:23*

"For the wages of sin is death." *Romans 6:23*

People have tried many ways to bridge this gap between themselves and God.

The Bible says...

"There is a way that seems right to a man, but its end is the way to death." *Proverbs 14:12*

"Your iniquities have made a separation between you and your God…" *Isaiah 59:2*

No bridge reaches God … except one.

Step 3. Discover God's bridge—the cross

Jesus Christ died on the cross and rose from the grave. Though he was God's sinless Son, he became a human, took our place, and paid the penalty for our sin, bridging the gap between God and us.

The Bible says…

"For there is one God, and there is one mediator between God and men, the man Christ Jesus." *1 Timothy 2:5*

"Christ … suffered once for sins, the righteous for the unrighteous, that he might bring us to God." *1 Peter 3:18*

"God shows his love for us in that while we were still sinners, Christ died for us … the free gift of God is eternal life in Christ Jesus our Lord." *Romans 5:8, 3:23*

"Christ died for our sins … he was buried … he was raised on the third day." *1 Corinthians 15:3-4*

God has provided the only way to forgiveness of sin and eternal life. But each person must make a choice.

Step 4. Embrace the truth—receive Christ

We must trust Jesus Christ as our Savior and receive him by personal choice.

Jesus says…

"Behold, I stand at the door and knock. If anyone hears my voice and opens the door, I will come in and eat with him, and he with me." *Revelation 3:20*

"I am the way, and the truth, and the life. No one comes to the Father except through me." *John 14:6*

The Bible says…

"To all who did receive him, who believed in his name, he gave the right to become children of God." *John 1:12*

"Whoever believes in the Son has eternal life." *John 3:36*

What is your decision?

Will you receive Jesus Christ right now and trust in him alone for forgiveness and eternal life? The Bible says that's the only way to find peace with God!

- Admit your need—that you are a sinner in need of God's forgiveness.
- Be willing to turn from trusting in anything else for eternal life and trust only in Christ.
- Believe that Jesus Christ died for you on the cross, came back to life from the grave, and is your only way to heaven.
- Accept Jesus' offer to forgive your sins and come into your life as your Savior.

You may want to tell him in words like these:

"Dear Jesus, thank you for making it possible for me to find peace with God! I believe that when you died you were paying the penalty for my sins. I now receive you into my life as my Savior, so I can have forgiveness and never-ending life from God! Thank you for the gift of eternal life!" [2]

Questions For Reflection And Discussion

1. Why does religious pluralism fail culturally, logically, Scripturally and truthfully?
2. Can we really know that we are going to Heaven?
3. What are the Steps to Peace with God?

NOTES:

---

[1] Billy Graham, *The Journey* (Nashville: W Publishing Group, 2006), 73.

[2] *Steps to Peace with God* witnessing tract, Crossway.org, published 2006, Good News Publishers and Crossway Books.

CONCLUSION

"Only one answer will give a person the certain privilege, the joy, of entering Heaven. Because I have believed in Jesus Christ and accepted Him as my Savior. He is the One sitting at the right hand of God and interceding for me. No one can deny the Christian his entrance into Heaven."[1] – Billy Graham

The Indian fable illustrated in chapter one about the elephant and the blind men was originally designed to illustrate that each religion is a part of the ultimate truth and leads to that truth by different roads. The misleading COEXIST bumper sticker so prevalent on cars all over town is sending the false message that all religions lead to the same spiritual truth. Hence, all roads lead to Heaven.

The coexist/interfaith movement has garnered so much attention that the National Geographic television network produced a six-part series on the subject in April of 2016 called *The Story of God* narrated by award winning actor Morgan Freeman. As a result of the advancement of such programming, we are seeing an increased number of media and social media campaigns pushing the coexist agenda as more folks than ever trade in their belief in the absolute truth about the biblical God for the false belief in religious pluralism. Religious pluralism *denies objective truth* about God and Heaven on one hand while *assuming objective truth* regarding its own pluralistic view concerning God and Heaven on the other. If this appears to be illogical and self-defeating, it is.

This is increasingly the way Christians are defining their walk with God as they are experiencing God primarily through the lens of *emotion,* with very little attention given to *reason.* Biblical Scripture is clear that we are to love the Lord our God with our heart and our mind. We must be careful not to overemphasize our heart experience of God and de-emphasize a right understanding of Him through our mind. It's not an *either/or.* It is *both/and.* Jesus said, "You shall love the Lord your God with all your heart and with all your soul and with all your mind" (Matthew 22:37). While our emotions are a legitimate factor regarding our faith in God and our walk with Jesus Christ, they ought not to be the primary way in which we understand God. Our emotions can change at any moment according to external factors, but God does not change. God is the same yesterday and today and forever (Hebrews 13:8). Today's world of *feel good/positive thinking* religious messages is due in part to the politically charged multi-cultural movement.

Within the context of discovering God, multi-culturalism is good as long as the different cultures unite under the Federal Headship of the true God. Religious pluralism's multi-cultural coexist message offers some level of immediate relief through the belief that one can drop the exclusivity of their faith in an attempt to restore cultural harmony. This is called *cognitive dissonance*—dropping the belief in Jesus Christ as the exclusive way to Heaven for the inclusive belief in religious pluralism in hopes of restoring mental harmony. Many folks are turning to *feel good* sermons in an effort to achieve peace in the face of ISIS, government pressure, and Christian persecution. While these feel good messages may mask the conflicts in the heart for the short term, they do nothing to truly relieve the trials or to resolve the issue of being eternally separated from God.

Religious pluralism is a diversionary tactic in the war against the truth about God and the coexist mantra a diversionary tactic for ushering in religious pluralism in the new age.

The New Age Movement's Effort To Redefine Jesus And The Truth About Heaven

Religious pluralism through the New Age Movement seeks to redefine Jesus Christ from man's perspective. This is made evident by the rise of the interfaith movement, which seeks to blend all religious faiths into a new false religion that feels and sounds good. NAM's pluralistic religion claims that all religions are equally true, that each provides a genuine encounter with the Ultimate, and it assumes that all roads lead to Heaven.[2] But NAM's presumptions are false and the New Age *interfaith* movement's mantra should be *contradict* instead of *coexist* because religious pluralism fails *biblically, in reality, logically, culturally,* and as *truth.*

Religious Pluralism Fails Biblically

The Bible, which is the most validated historical ancient document in all of history, affirms that Jesus Christ claimed to be the only way to Heaven. "I am the way and the truth and the life. No one comes to the Father except through me (John 14:6). Earlier, in chapter 10, Jesus had boldly proclaimed that anyone who tries to get to Heaven through any other way than by Him is a thief, "I tell you the truth, the man who does not enter the sheep pen by the gate, but climbs in by some other way, is a thief and a robber ... I am the gate; whoever enters through me will be saved" (John 10:1, 9). When we look into the Old Testament Scriptures we get an idea of what God thinks about man worshipping false gods. "But if you or your sons turn away from me and do not observe the commands and decrees I have given you and go off to serve other gods and worship them, then I will cut off Israel form the land I have given them ... " (1 Kings 9:6-7).

The Biblical account of Jesus differs greatly from the Jesus of the New Age Movement (NAM). The original ancient Jewish Scriptures and Christian New Testament manuscripts speak quite differently about Jesus than NAM's pluralistic assertions regarding the person, life, and return of Jesus Christ. First, the Christ of the Bible calls the Christ of NAM an Antichrist (1John 2:18; 2:22; 4:3; 2 John 1:7). Second, the Bible tells us that Christ will return just as He ascended, visibly and personally. "Men of Galilee," they said, "why do you stand here looking into the sky? This same Jesus, who has been taken from you into heaven, will come back in the same way you have seen him go into heaven" (Acts 1:11). Jesus will return personally, in bodily form, not technologically by way of computers or video (Mt. 24:29-38; Acts 1:11).

Third, NAM asserts that Jesus the Christ did not resurrect from the dead but was reincarnated as a higher spiritual entity. NAM holds that He did not conquer death since in His new manifestation He would logically die again. Some NAM believers think Jesus has not finished reincarnating, that He has merged into the impersonal godhead, obliterating the *person* of Jesus Christ.[3] The Bible on the other hand tells us that when Christ returns, He will do so *personally*, and in such a way that *all* will recognize Him (Matt 24:7). Lastly, Jesus Christ is clearly and unmistakably the unique one and only Messiah, not the NAM-fabricated finite god or merely a prophet, enlightened master, or a spiritual guide.[4]

Religious Pluralism Fails In Reality

The world's religions have coexisted for centuries. The coexist bumper sticker implies that all religions lead to the same spiritual truth and that all roads lead to Heaven, which is different than all religions simply getting along. To illustrate this point, let's look at Islam. In places like Saudi Arabia, Iran, and most all of the Middle East where Islamic Sharia law rules, there is no tolerance for religious pluralism. In the Middle East, it is illegal to believe in Jesus Christ as *God*, start a Christian church, or practice any religion outside of orthodox Islam. To share your faith or preach the Christian faith is a capital offense in this part of the world. For example, Pastor Saeed Abedini, who was released from prison in January of 2016, said that, like many Christians as well as Sunni Muslims, he was charged with the typical conviction of what the Islamic regime considers as a threat to national security, espionage, or trying to overthrow the government.[5] Pastor Abedini's crime was that he started an orphanage in Iran in addition to sharing his Christian faith. Because Islam is a theocracy, the government, military, court/legal system and religion are all inseparable. Does this look like Islam is tolerant of religious pluralism?

Throughout history, Islam has proven to tolerate religious pluralism and any other religion just long enough to gain the influence and power it needs to assume government control through the democratic process or by force. The Quran says in Sura 8, "Fight them until all are Muslims. *And fight with them until there is no more persecution, and all religions are for Allah* (Sura 8:40). The state of religious liberty that Islam aims at can be put tersely into two opening statements: There is no more persecution and All religions are for Allah.[6] The Quran calls for Muslims not to coexist peacefully with non-Muslims but to make war against unbelievers (non-Muslims) until they recant their faith and become Muslim: *Fight those who believe not in Allah nor in the Last Day, nor forbid that which Allah and His Messenger have forbidden nor follow the Religion of Truth, out of those who have been given the Book, until they pay the tax in acknowledgment of superiority and they are in a state of subjection* (Surah 9:29).[7]

We can make a similar argument for each different religion—that religious pluralism fails in reality, because it contradicts the individual beliefs of each of those religions. In reality, every religion believes that they have the truth and that all of the other religions' claims are false regarding being the true religion, having the true God, and knowing the true salvific path to Heaven.

Religious Pluralism Fails Logically

Third, pluralism fails *logically* because it denies the logical laws called *first principles*. First Principles of logic are called such because there is nothing behind them and it is through them that we discover truths about the world. For example, the logical *law of identity* states that *a thing must be identical to itself or it would not be itself.* You and I have a unique identity; no two of us are exactly alike. This is true for all *beings*, including identical twins, cloned creatures, and God Himself.

The Tech Museum of Innovation in San Jose, Calif., posted an article on October 24, 2005, saying that even when animals have been cloned there are differences. Genetic Savings and Clone, Inc., cloned the first cat in 2001 and in 2005 the first dog was cloned. Not only were the clones not exactly the same as the originals, but they also had different personalities.[8] In other words, they did not share the exact same *identity*. We as human beings have unique fingerprints and DNA. This testifies to our unique identity. The same is true of the *uniqueness* of Jesus Christ as the true God from eternity. The law of identity applies to Jesus Christ uniquely as the second person in the Godhead, and it applies also to various world religions. The law of identity eliminates religious pluralism and the contention that all roads lead to Heaven. The person of God and every religion must be identical to itself or it would not in fact be itself. If God is not identical to Himself, He in fact is not God. If any religion is not identical to itself, it is in fact not that religion.

Because each religion has its own unique identity, it is recognizable as its own unique entity from the beginning. We are for example only able to differentiate between Islam, Hinduism, and Christianity due to their *identity*. If any two religions were 100 percent the same in their traditions, theology, and their understanding of God, they would in fact be the same religion. The coexist mantra of religious pluralism is saying the exact opposite in attempting to meld very different identities into one thing. This is like attempting to force a square peg into a round hole. The same is true of God. If the monotheistic God of Islam, which denies the Christian Trinity, and the hundreds of millions of gods found in Hinduism and Christian Scriptures all shared the same identity, they would all be identifiable as the same exact God. But they are not; they are so radically different that it is impossible to meld them into one identifiable religion. Each religion has its own very different and opposing identity. Because Jesus Christ, Muhammad, and the many gods of Hinduism all carry different identities, it follows that the religions they represent fails to complement each other, but rather contradicts each other. If all religions held the same exact identity we wouldn't be having discussion about the coexist message of religious pluralism.

Another logical First Principle is the *Law of Noncontradiction*. This first principle law of logic says that opposite ideas cannot both be true and not true at the same time and in the same sense. This means that Islam, Hinduism, and Christianity cannot all be the truth at the same *time* and in the same *sense*.[9] See the following contradictions between Islam and Christianity.

1) *Muhammad* was not virgin born, but ***Jesus*** was.
2) *Muhammad* was sinful, but ***Jesus*** was sinless.
3) *Muhammad* never did miracles, but ***Jesus*** did many miracles.

4) *Muhammad* used the sword to establish Islam as a religion. *Jesus* forbids the sword in spreading Christianity (Matt. 26:52).
5) *Muhammad* retaliated against his enemies, *Jesus* forgave His enemies.
6) *Muhammad* motivated people by fear, *Jesus* motivated people by love.
7) *Muhammad* was overcome by death, *Jesus* overcame death.

The Medieval Muslim philosopher Avicenna said, "Anyone who denies the Law of Noncontradiction should be beaten and burned until he admits that to be beaten is not the same as not to be beaten, and to be burned is not the same as not to be burned!"[10] Does this sound like support for the coexist bumper sticker or tolerance regarding religious pluralism?

To have an identity means to have a single identity, and an object or a religion cannot have two identities—that would be a contradiction. The claim that all religions ultimately lead to the same spiritual truth still connotes a *singular, exclusive truth claim.* Logic mandates that there must be only one truth, and to be *the truth* makes all other definitions of God, and all other roads to Heaven, false.

Religious Pluralism Fails Culturally

Fourth, religious pluralism fails *culturally* because it denies each culture its own unique traditions and cultural beliefs. Anyone who doesn't believe this should try going to a local Mosque to tell the Muslim

Imam that Christ is equal to Muhammad or that Jesus is an optional path to Allah in taking one to Heaven. This would be culturally offensive to the Islamic faith and contradictory to the Muslim culture.

Or, try asking an atheist to accept the fact that Jesus Christ will take him or her to Heaven. Atheism does not take a culturally neutral position. It rather denies every world religion its beliefs about God. If an Atheist were to go into a Hindu Temple, an Islamic Mosque, or a Christian Church and argue their position that there *is no God*—neither *theistic* (one God who created all) nor *pantheistic* (god is all)—the Atheist would be denying the other faiths their cultural traditions as well as their individual religious beliefs about God, salvation, and eternity.

Religious Pluralism Fails Truthfully

Finally, religious pluralism fails in truth. While rejection of the truth has been held as a belief by some throughout world history, the rejection of truth by mainstream culture didn't take a foothold in American culture until the 1960's. In the sixties a rebellious generation questioned authority—the authority of God, government, military, parents, the person of Jesus Christ, and absolute truth itself. Decades after the rebellious 1960's, we are feeling the grave consequences of multiple generation's perpetual rejection of authority and the denial of Jesus as God. For the first time in American history, most of mainstream culture either does not understand the nature of truth, or it rejects truth as absolute. Because of this, most people are unable to understand or identify who or what God truly *is* and what He *is not*.

The importance of the *nature* of truth is critical to all people, especially those in the Christian faith because Christianity claims that there is *absolute truth* for everyone, everywhere, at all times. Jesus tells us that all roads do not lead to Heaven. It is true for every person who has ever lived, or who is yet to be born, that Jesus said, "I tell you the truth, the man who does not enter the sheep pen by the gate, but climbs in by some other way, is a thief and a robber" (John 10:1). If you deny the concept of truth, it logically follows that you cannot know the truth about God. As stated earlier in this book, truth is *what corresponds to reality*, it's *telling it as it is*, and it simply is *what is*. Christianity claims that truth about the world and reality is that which corresponds to *the way things really are*. If those who hold to *religious pluralism* were to acknowledge that truth is absolute, then they would be able to discern the truth of God. Religious pluralism is a spiritual, diversionary tactic in the war against the truth of God. It is an effort to redefine Him according to culture or personal taste.

The Options For False Gods Are Limitless

With religious pluralism, the options for false gods are limitless. Mark Twain said, "Truth is stranger than fiction, but it is because Fiction is obliged to stick to possibilities. Truth isn't."[11] The battle for the truth about God is the Lord's (1 Samuel 17:47), and we must remember the enemy is the devil, not the person we are speaking with (Matthew 13:37-39). False ideas give apparent justification for a false understanding of the true God.

It is one thing to make up false assertions that feel good, but another to give a truthful reason for God and Heaven. The human mind and emotions often seek the path of least resistance. There are limit-less options in choosing a god to follow, but only belief in the true God will lead to the one true road to Heaven.

Jesus proclaimed, "I am the way and the truth and the life. No one comes to the Father except through Me" (John 14:6). My prayer is that this book has helped you discover the true God of the universe in Jesus Christ, or that it has increased your faith in Jesus Christ by help-ing you see for yourself that all religions don't lead to Heaven. The next time you see the COEXIST bumper sticker, please ponder the things that we have discussed in this book. It would be more honest for the COEXIST bumper sticker to change its mantra to CONTRADICT. It is when we look at the facts, when we examine the pluralist argu-ments through the lens of truth, and accurately study the historical data found in biblical Scriptures, that we are able to clearly discern the truth—the truth that there is only one true God and only one true road to Heaven.

Now this is eternal life: that they know you, the only true God, and Jesus Christ, whom you have sent (John 17:3).

NOTES:

[1] Billy Graham, *Facing Death and the Life After,* (Waco, TX: Word, 1987), 216.

[2] Norman L. Geisler, *Bakers Encyclopedia of Christian Apologetics*, (Grand Rapids, MI: Baker Books, Fourth Printing, June 2000), 598.

[3] John Ankerberg & John Weldon, *Encyclopedia of New Age Beliefs*, (Eugene, OR: Harvest House Publishers, 1996), 673.

[4] Ankerberg, *The Facts On The New Age Movement, Answers to the 30 most frequently asked questions about the New Age Movement (Eugene, OR: Harvest House Publishers, 1988)*, 22.

[5] http://www.jns.org/latest-articles/2016/1/29/as-iran-frees-american-pastor-persecution-of-iranian-christians-rages-on-1#.Vq4OarIrLIU=

[6] Maulana Muhammad Ali, *The Holy Quran with English Translation and Commentary*, New 2002 edition, (Dublin, OH: Ahmadiyya Anjuman Isha 'at Islam Lahore Inc., U.S.A., 2002), 385.

[7] Maulana Muhammad Ali, *The Holy Quran*, 403-404.

[8] The Tech Museum of Innovation-Stanford at Tech Understanding Genetics, *Cloning*. October 24, 2005. http://genetics.thetech.org/ask/ask147

[9] Winfried Corduan, *A Christian Introduction to World Religions Neighboring Faiths*, (Downers Grove, IL: InterVarsity Press, 1998), 189.

[10] Norman L. Geisler, *I Don't Have Enough Faith to Be an Atheist*, (Wheaton, IL: Crossway Books, 2004), 57.

[11] Mark Twain, *Following the Equator: A Journey Around the World, Pudd'nhead Wilson's New Calendar*, http://www.twainquotes.com/Truth.html

CONTACT Steven

Steven speaks frequently on the topic of *Theology, Apologetics and using apologetics in evangelism.* He can deliver a keynote, partial day, half-day, or full-day version of this content, depending on your needs. If you are interested in finding out more, please contact Steven at: http://reasonfortruth.org/equippedseminars/host-a-seminar

You can also connect with Steven here:

Facebook: https://www.facebook.com/NationalApologeticsTraini ngCenter/?ref=bookmarks

Twitter: https://twitter.com/steve_garofalo

Web Site: ReasonForTruth.Org

To Subscribe to the *Reason For Truth* Podcast, go to http://reasonfor-truth.org/podcast-video